MATH PHONICS™

SUBTRACTION

Quick Tips and Alternative Techniques for Math Mastery

BY MARILYN B. HEIN

ILLUSTRATED BY RON WHEELER

Teaching & Learning Company

1204 Buchanan St., P.O. Box 10

Carthage, IL 62321-0010

THIS BOOK BELONGS TO

____

ACKNOWLEDGEMENTS

I appreciate the support given to me by Cindy Goodwin, Joanne Hampton and Jeanne Ast. Thanks to Sarah, Rachel and Hannah Minson for field testing math games. Special thanks to Laura Meyer for all she taught me.

DEDICATION

I would like to dedicate this book to my husband, Joe; our children, Gretchen, Troy, Adam, Sarah, Robert, Nick and Jenny; and my parents, Vincent and Cleora Vestring.

Cover by Ron Wheeler

ISBN No. 1-57310-096-X

Printing No. 987654321

Teaching & Learning Company
1204 Buchanan St., P.O. Box 10
Carthage, IL 62321-0010

TABLE OF CONTENTS

NOTE TO PARENTS

Although this book has been specifically designed to be used by classroom teachers for teaching subtraction facts, the materials are extremely helpful when used by parents and children at home.

If you have purchased this book to use at home with your child, I recommend that all of the fill-in-the-blank pages be inserted into vinyl page protectors and worked with a dry-erase overhead transparency marker. The page protectors can be washed and the page can be reused. Put all the page protectors and worksheets into a vinyl, two-pocket binder. The pen, flash cards and other materials can be kept in the binder pockets, thus creating a handy, portable math kit.

I think you will find that these methods work extremely well both at home and in the classroom. They have been tested and approved by parents and teachers!

Dear Teacher or Parent,

True or false?

1. Learning math is hard work.
2. Learning math is fun.

Both true! It is very rare to find someone who can really do well in math without putting in a lot of time doing homework to practice what has been learned, drilling important facts and reviewing for tests.

But at the same time, with a little creativity, we can always come up with some fun ways to demonstrate a new concept, drill the memory work and review the important material. Mathematics is a part of every aspect of our lives. Anyone who enjoys life can share that zest for life while teaching math!

From spending time with my own six children, seeing what types of games and activities they enjoy, I have designed these *Math Phonics™* books from the angle of fun mixed with the hard work.

Take a look at the varied worksheets, board game, card games and classroom games for drill. Take a look at the short, easy-to-learn rules which make this approach so much like language arts phonics. Take a look at the take-home materials which involve the parents and help them keep in touch with their children. Take a look at the students' faces when they realize they have mastered 101 subtraction facts!

We hear a lot about building self-esteem these days. Good teachers have always known how to build self-esteem–challenge your students, teach them to work hard, help them when they need some extra support, involve parents so students get some one-on-one attention, praise them for their hard work, let them know when they have done a good job and have some fun once in a while!

So dive in, take a look at what I'm offering you, work hard and please have some fun.

Sincerely,

Marilyn

Marilyn B. Hein

WHAT IS MATH PHONICS™?

Math Phonics™ is a specially designed program for teaching subtraction facts initially or for remedial work.

WHY IS IT CALLED MATH PHONICS™?

In reading, phonics is used to group similar words, and it teaches the students simple rules for pronouncing each word.

In *Math Phonics*™, math facts are grouped and learned by means of simple patterns, rules and mnemonic devices.

In reading, phonics develops mastery by repetitive use of words already learned.

Math Phonics™ uses drill and review to reinforce students' understanding.

HOW WAS MATH PHONICS™ DEVELOPED?

Why did "Johnny" have so much trouble learning to read during the years that phonics was dropped from the curriculum of many schools in this country? For the most part, he had to simply memorize every single word in order to learn to read, an overwhelming task for a young child. If he had an excellent memory or a knack for noticing patterns in words, he had an easier time of it. If he lacked those skills, learning to read was a nightmare, often ending in failure–failure to learn to read and failure in school.

Phonics seems to help many children learn to read more easily. Why? When a young child learns one phonics rule, that one rule unlocks the pronunciation of dozens or even hundreds of words. It also provides the key to parts of many larger words. The trend in U.S. schools today seems to be to include phonics in the curriculum because of the value of that particular system of learning.

As a substitute teacher, I have noticed that math teacher manuals sometimes have some valuable phonics-like memory tools for teachers to share with students to help them memorize math facts–the addition, subtraction, multiplication and division facts which are the building blocks of arithmetic. However, much of what I remembered from my own education was not contained in the available materials. I decided to create my own materials based upon what I had learned during the past 40 years as a student, teacher and parent.

The name *Math Phonics*™ occurred to me because the rules, patterns and memory techniques that I have assembled are similar to language arts phonics in several ways. Most of these rules are short and easy to learn. Children are taught to look for patterns and use them as "crutches" for coming up with the answer quickly. Some groups have similarities so that learning one group makes it easier to learn another. Last of all, *Math Phonics*™ relies on lots of drill and review, just as language arts phonics does.

Children *must* master addition, subtraction, multiplication and division facts and the sooner the better. When I taught seventh and eighth grade math over 20 years ago, I was amazed at the number of students who had not mastered the basic math facts. At that time, I had no idea how to help them. My college math classes did not give me any preparation for that situation. I had not yet delved into my personal memory bank to try to remember how I had mastered those facts.

When my six children had problems in that area, I was strongly motivated to give some serious thought to the topic. I knew my children had to master math facts, and I needed to come up with additional ways to help them. For kids to progress past the lower grades without a thorough knowledge of those facts would be like trying to learn to read without knowing the alphabet.

I have always marveled at the large number of people who tell me that they "hated math" when they were kids. I wonder how many of them struggled with the basic math facts when they needed to have them clearly in mind. I firmly believe that a widespread use of *Math Phonics*™ could be a tremendous help in solving the problem of "math phobia."

WHAT ARE THE PRINCIPLES OF MATH PHONICS™?

There are three underlying principles of *Math Phonics*™.

They are:
1. Understanding
2. Learning
3. Mastery

Here is a brief explanation of the meaning of these principles.

1. UNDERSTANDING: All true mathematical concepts are abstract which means they can't be touched. They exist in the mind. For most of us, understanding such concepts is much easier if they can be related to something in the real world–something that can be touched.

Thus I encourage teachers and parents to find answers for themselves using small objects, number lines and counting charts. I think this helps the students to remember answers once they have discovered them on their own.

2. LEARNING: Here is where the rules and patterns mentioned earlier play an important part. A child can be taught a simple rule and on the basis of that, call to mind a whole set of math facts. But the learning necessary for the addition, subtraction, multiplication and division facts must be firmly in place so that the information will be remembered next week, next month and several years from now. That brings us to the next principle.

3. MASTERY: We have all had the experience of memorizing some information for a test or quiz tomorrow and then promptly forgetting most of it. This type of memorization will not work for the math facts. In order for children to master these facts, *Math Phonics*™ provides visual illustrations, wall charts, flash cards, practice sheets, worksheets and games. Some children may only need one or two of these materials, but there are plenty from which to choose for those who need more.

POCKET FOLDERS

You will want to purchase or create a pocket folder for each student to keep all the *Math Phonics*™ materials together.

Inexpensive pocket folders are available at many school or office supply stores, discount stores or other outlets.

An easy-to-make pocket folder can be made from a large paper grocery or shopping bag.

1. Cut away the bottom of the bag and discard.

2. Cut open along one long side and lay flat.

3. Pick one of the folds and measure out 10" (25 cm) from the fold on either side. Trim bag.

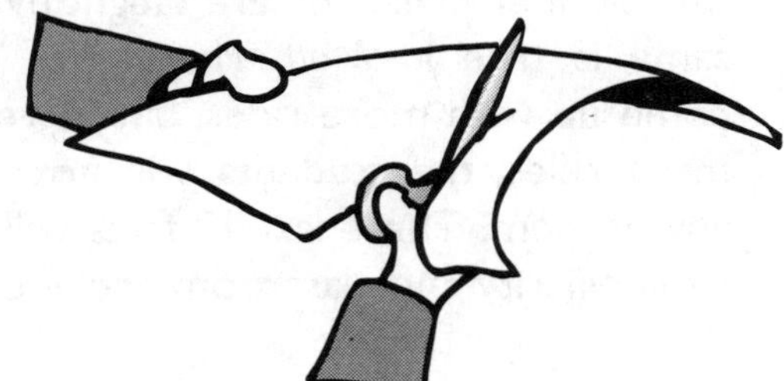

4. Now measure 12" (30 cm) down from the top and fold up the remaining portion of the bag.

5. Staple pockets at outside edges and fold in half.

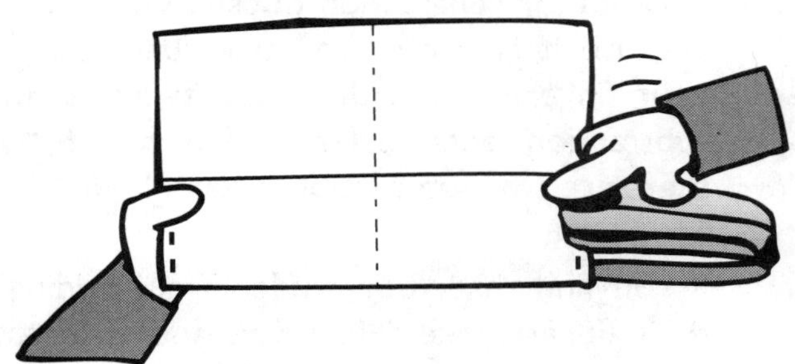

6. Decorate front and back.

Suggest to parents that children should keep all of their *Math Phonics*™ materials (worksheets, travel folders, progress charts, etc.) in this folder. Parents may also wish to supply clear plastic page protectors and dry-erase markers. Worksheets can be inserted into the page protectors, completed with the dry-erase marker and reused. (See note on page 14.)

SUMMARY OF THE 10 BASIC STEPS

1. Understanding Subtraction

This is a brief but very important step. We need to be sure that all students understand exactly what is meant by the word *subtraction*. Most do, but some may not.

2. Relating Subtraction to Addition

If students have mastered addition and understand how subtraction builds on addition, learning subtraction is made much easier.

I believe that many people add on their fingers throughout their lives. They may do this mentally, but they are still counting out the answer rather than memorizing the fact. Counting out answers for subtraction doesn't work so well, because it is harder to count backwards on your fingers. Also, there are twice as many subtraction facts to learn. For 5 + 6 = 11, there are two subtraction facts: 11 - 6 = 5 and 11 - 5 = 6.

If you find that your students are adding on their fingers, take a few days and go through the *Math Phonics™–Addition* book with its easy-to-learn rules and patterns. It will pay off in speed and accuracy in adding, and it will help students learn subtraction.

3. Addition Doubles as Subtraction Problems

Addition doubles are equations such as 2 + 2 = 4, 3 + 3 = 6 and so on. These will be changed into subtraction problems and learned first. 4 - 2 = 2; 6 - 3 = 3 and so on. This group is learned first because knowing it well is a tremendous help in learning the 2s in multiplication and division.

4. Subtracting Number Neighbors and Subtracting 1

If you have not used *Math Phonics™–Addition*, you will need to explain the idea of number neighbors–two numbers side-by-side on the number line–6 and 5, for example. When you subtract number neighbors, the answer is always one (6 - 5 = 1). When you subtract one, the answer is always the smaller number neighbor (6 - 1 = 5). These two facts are also called matching facts because they use the same three numbers.

5. Subtracting 0 and Matching Facts

These will be simple to teach, but it pays to spend a little time on them. Zero can be confusing, because its effects are different in multiplication and division than in addition and subtraction.

6. Subtracting 9 and Matching Facts

This will be simplified for students by use of a simple rule. One of the 9s' facts is 11 - 9 = 2. Its matching fact is 11 - 2 = 9.

7. Subtracting 2 and Matching Facts

These groups will also be taught by using a simple rule.

8. Number Pairs for 7, 8 and 9

There are eight facts included in this step which will be taught by reviewing addition facts and relating the subtraction facts to addition.

9. Number Pairs for 10 and 11

The 10 facts in this step will also be taught by review of addition and several classroom activities.

10. Last 12 Facts

In language arts phonics, after all rules have been learned, there are several words which do not fit any rule and are taught by rote. The same is true in *Math Phonics™*. We could come up with more rules, but if we have too many rules, the students will not remember any of them. These last 12 facts will be taught by familiarity and classroom activities.

SUBTRACTION FACTS

Facts in boxes are matching facts.

Doubles

- 2 - 1 = 1
- 4 - 2 = 2
- 6 - 3 = 3
- 8 - 4 = 4
- 10 - 5 = 5
- 12 - 6 = 6
- 14 - 7 = 7
- 16 - 8 = 8
- 18 - 9 = 9

Number Neighbors

- 10 - 9 = 1
- 9 - 8 = 1
- 8 - 7 = 1
- 7 - 6 = 1
- 6 - 5 = 1
- 5 - 4 = 1
- 4 - 3 = 1
- 3 - 2 = 1
- 2 - 1 = 1

Number Neighbors

- 10 - 1 = 9
- 9 - 1 = 8
- 8 - 1 = 7
- 7 - 1 = 6
- 6 - 1 = 5
- 5 - 1 = 4
- 4 - 1 = 3
- 3 - 1 = 2
- 2 - 1 = 1

0s

- 0 - 0 = 0
- 1 - 0 = 1
- 2 - 0 = 2
- 3 - 0 = 3
- 4 - 0 = 4
- 5 - 0 = 5
- 6 - 0 = 6
- 7 - 0 = 7
- 8 - 0 = 8
- 9 - 0 = 9
- 10 - 0 = 10

0s

- 0 - 0 = 0
- 1 - 1 = 0
- 2 - 2 = 0
- 3 - 3 = 0
- 4 - 4 = 0
- 5 - 5 = 0
- 6 - 6 = 0
- 7 - 7 = 0
- 8 - 8 = 0
- 9 - 9 = 0
- 10 - 10 = 0

9s

- 10 - 9 = 1
- 11 - 9 = 2
- 12 - 9 = 3
- 13 - 9 = 4
- 14 - 9 = 5
- 15 - 9 = 6
- 16 - 9 = 7
- 17 - 9 = 8
- 18 - 9 = 9

9s

- 10 - 1 = 9
- 11 - 2 = 9
- 12 - 3 = 9
- 13 - 4 = 9
- 14 - 5 = 9
- 15 - 6 = 9
- 16 - 7 = 9
- 17 - 8 = 9
- 18 - 9 = 9

2s

- 11 - 2 = 9
- 9 - 2 = 7
- 7 - 2 = 5
- 5 - 2 = 3
- 3 - 2 = 1
- 10 - 2 = 8
- 8 - 2 = 6
- 6 - 2 = 4
- 4 - 2 = 2

2s

- 11 - 9 = 2
- 9 - 7 = 2
- 7 - 5 = 2
- 5 - 3 = 2
- 3 - 1 = 2
- 10 - 8 = 2
- 8 - 6 = 2
- 6 - 4 = 2
- 4 - 2 = 2

Number Pairs for 7

- 7 - 1 = 6
- 7 - 2 = 5
- 7 - 3 = 4
- 7 - 4 = 3
- 7 - 5 = 2
- 7 - 6 = 1

Number Pairs for 8

- 8 - 1 = 7
- 8 - 2 = 6
- 8 - 3 = 5
- 8 - 4 = 4
- 8 - 5 = 3
- 8 - 6 = 2
- 8 - 7 = 1

Number Pairs for 9

- 9 - 1 = 8
- 9 - 2 = 7
- 9 - 3 = 6
- 9 - 4 = 5
- 9 - 5 = 4
- 9 - 6 = 3
- 9 - 7 = 2
- 9 - 8 = 1

Number Pairs for 10

- 10 - 1 = 9
- 10 - 2 = 8
- 10 - 3 = 7
- 10 - 4 = 6
- 10 - 5 = 5
- 10 - 6 = 4
- 10 - 7 = 3
- 10 - 8 = 2
- 10 - 9 = 1

Number Pairs for 11

- 11 - 2 = 9
- 11 - 3 = 8
- 11 - 4 = 7
- 11 - 5 = 6
- 11 - 6 = 5
- 11 - 7 = 4
- 11 - 8 = 3
- 11 - 9 = 2

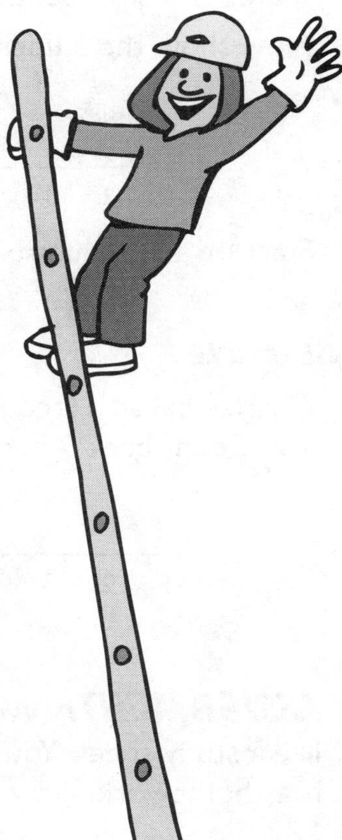

Number Pairs for 12

- 12 - 3 = 9
- 12 - 4 = 8
- 12 - 5 = 7
- 12 - 6 = 6
- 12 - 7 = 5
- 12 - 8 = 4
- 12 - 9 = 3

Number Pairs for 13

- 13 - 4 = 9
- 13 - 5 = 8
- 13 - 6 = 7
- 13 - 7 = 6
- 13 - 8 = 5
- 13 - 9 = 4

Number Pairs for 14

- 14 - 5 = 9
- 14 - 6 = 8
- 14 - 7 = 7
- 14 - 8 = 6
- 14 - 9 = 5

Number Pairs for 15

- 15 - 6 = 9
- 15 - 7 = 8
- 15 - 8 = 7
- 15 - 9 = 6

LESSON PLAN 1

OBJECTIVE: Understanding subtraction. Students will understand the meaning of the word *subtraction* and why it is important in our lives.

MATERIALS: Worksheet A (page 12), purchase a wall-size number line or enlarge and laminate the one in this book (page 13), parents' note (page 14), Optional Notes (page 15)

INTRODUCTION: Write the word *subtraction* on the board. Have the students memorize the spelling of the word. Break it into three syllables:

SUB: This is exactly the way it sounds.

TRAC: Point out that the K sound is spelled with the letter C.

TION: This is a common ending syllable.

Explain that this is a way of keeping track of a number of objects after some have been taken away.

It is very important to use concrete examples so students will understand exactly what *subtraction* means.

EXAMPLE 1:

Jane has $15.00. She buys a model rocket kit for $8.00. How much money does she have left? Write on the board: 15 - 8 = ?

Have 15 students stand up. They are the 15 dollars. Count eight and have them sit down. They are the dollars she spent. Count how many are left–7. They answer is: 15 - 8 = 7.

Now show the students how to find the answer on a number line.

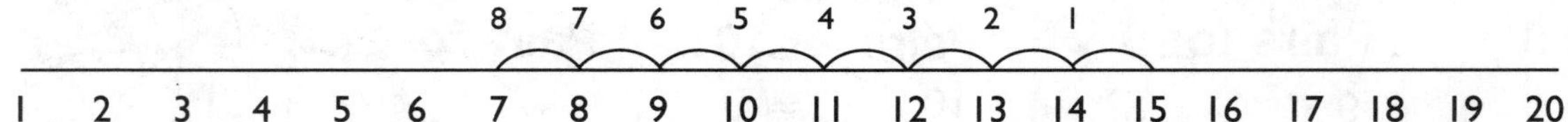

Start on 15. Count back 8 numbers. The answer is 7.

EXAMPLE 2:

Charles baked 16 cookies. His friends ate 9. How many are left? Use the number line. Start on 16. Count back 9 numbers. The answer is 16 - 9 = 7.

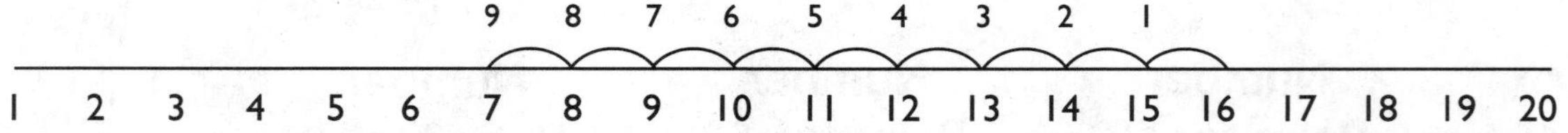

ASSIGNMENT: Worksheet A. This is more like a study sheet. You can do it as a class or give it as homework.

LESSON PLAN 1

TAKE-HOME: Students should interview parents or friends to learn how subtraction is used in the world. Tell them to especially ask about money. Students need to know how important it is for a person to be able to subtract to know how much change they will be getting when they pay for something, or how much money they have in the bank. Bankers and clerks sometimes make mistakes and once in a great while we run into a dishonest person who tries to cheat us out of our money. Nobody wants to be robbed. Sometimes we protect ourselves by calling the police. Sometimes we protect ourselves by knowing how to SUBTRACT!

On the back of Worksheet A, have students write at least three ways subtraction is used by their parents or friends.

PARENTS' NOTE: Send home parents' note. Read Optional Notes and use them if you wish.

ENRICHMENT: Thousands of years ago, people who couldn't read or write knew how to keep track of their belongings by adding and subtracting. If they didn't write down numbers, they might have kept pebbles in a leather pouch to keep track of the number of their sheep. Ancient Chinese used short sticks as counters–some Native Americans used shells. (*Golden Book Encyclopedia*, Vol. 11, p. 1012, Golden Press, New York.) We could still do this today, but written numbers are much easier. Imagine that you had 1,000 sheep, or earned a $1,000 a month. It would be very difficult to carry around 1,000 pebbles in your pocket, but you could write 1,000 in your record book or checkbook and subtract when the number changed.

Some students might ask why they have to learn to subtract since they can use a calculator. Tell them that although calculators are good, we don't always have one with us and batteries can wear out. We need to be able to do things without a machine–depending on a machine can sometimes cause big problems.

Name ___________________________________

Use this number line to find the answers.

0 1 2 3 4 5 6 7 8 9 10 11 12 13 14 15 16 17 18 19 20

1. **3 - 2 =** ______ 2. **5 - 1 =** ______ 3. **4 - 3 =** ______

4. **10 - 8 =** ______ 5. **9 - 6 =** ______ 6. **6 - 3 =** ______

7. **7 - 2 =** ______ 8. **9 - 2 =** ______ 9. **20 - 18 =** ______

10. **11 - 8 =** ______ 11. **12 - 6 =** ______ 12. **10 - 1 =** ______

13. **12 - 4 =** ______ 14. **14 - 7 =** ______ 15. **16 - 7 =** ______

16. Sarah lost her crayons. There were 8 in the box. She found 6. How many are still lost?
17. Sarah has a new box of 16 crayons. She gave 7 to her friend. How many of the new crayons does she have left from this box?
18. Sarah gave away 2 more crayons. Now how many are left from the box of 16?
19. Copy the word *subtraction* on the back five times.
20. Ask an adult how subtraction is used in the world. Write three answers on the back of this page.

CHALLENGE:
Sarah's friends gave her back the crayons from the box of 16. She got a box of 32 and a box of 64. She lost 5 crayons from each of the three boxes. How many crayons does she have in all from these three boxes?

NUMBER LINE

0 1 2 3 4 5 6 7 8 9 10 11 12 13 14 15 16 17 18 19 20

DEAR PARENTS,

Within the next few days our class will start to learn subtraction using the Math Phonics™ program. This program is set up in such a way that your help is necessary in order for your child to master the 101 subtraction facts. Your child MUST learn to subtract in order to succeed in math. Here are some things you can do to help.

1. Help your child find a good place to post the Travel Folders that will be sent home. Some kids learn better by seeing the facts than by learning them. Travel Folders could be put on the bathroom mirror, side of the fridge or on the wall near the light switch–anywhere that your child will see them several times a day.
2. Quiz your child verbally from time to time while you are fixing supper or driving in the car.
3. When your son or daughter can say a group of facts correctly, sign the space on the progress chart which will be sent home in a few days.
4. Review earlier groups once a week or so.
5. Use the flash cards which are sent home. You can also use them with a Trivial Pursuit™ board or other board game. Have your child show you card games which have been taught in school.
6. We need some sets of dice, dominoes and decks of playing cards. Could you donate any of these? Only send items which you do not want returned, as some pieces could be lost? Thanks!

Keep all *Math Phonics™* materials together so that your child can find them easily. Since the Math Phonics™ program relies on drill and review, we really need your help at home.

Sincerely,

OPTIONAL NOTES

Dear Parents,

The *Math Phonics*™ training meeting will be held:

Date ____________________

Time ____________________

Place ____________________

The meeting will be over in 30 minutes, but you may stay a little longer if you have questions.

Sincerely,

Dear Parents,

Your child is doing very well on the subtraction facts. He or she needs to especially work on these groups of facts:

Please continue working with your child on the drills and reviews. Students who do not learn subtraction now will have trouble with math in the future.

Sincerely,

Dear Parents,

Your child has mastered the 101 subtraction facts at this time. Congratulations! Be sure to continue to review these facts because without review, kids will forget them.

Sincerely,

If you are interested in attending a short training meeting for further information about *Math Phonics*™, please fill out this form and return to school tomorrow.

Name: ____________________

Phone No.:____________________

I am free these weekday evenings: ______________________________

LESSON PLAN 2

OBJECTIVE: Relating subtraction to addition. Students will understand the relationship between subtraction and addition. They will begin to use the addition facts they already know to find subtraction answers.

MATERIALS: Number Line (page 13), Addition Assessment (page 17), Worksheets B and C (pages 18 and 19)

INTRODUCTION: Students should share the subtraction examples they brought. Tell them they will be using subtraction later in the year in this class and in nearly every other math topic.

Check to be sure that students recall all the addition facts. Use the assessment page included in this book or another addition assessment. For any facts that are missed, use materials from *Math Phonics™–Addition* or other materials for review. For students who need extra help, find parents or older students who can help.

Students must know the addition facts before learning the subtraction facts.

HOMEWORK: Use Worksheets B and C.

HINT: When word problems or Challenge problems have several numbers, encourage students to draw a picture to help in solving the problem.

SUBTRACTION DEMONSTRATION: This will show students that addition and subtraction are opposites of each other. This will help them use their knowledge of addition in finding subtraction answers.

Jim and Ed each have 5 model cars that they are entering in the 4-H fair. All their cars will be on the same display table. How many cars do they have on their display table?

5 + 5 = 10

When the fair is over, Jim leaves first, taking his cars with him. How many are left? Find the answer on the number line if necessary.

10 - 5 = 5

Jan and Kim are putting their money together to buy a gift for their teacher. Kim has $7.00, and Jan has $9.00. How much money do they have together? Use a number line if necessary.

7 + 9 = 16

Jan remembers that she needs to save her money for the class trip. She takes her money and goes home. How much money is left?

16 - 9 = 7

What if Kim had been the one to go home first? How much money would have been left?

16 - 7 = 9

Be sure the students see that for every addition problem, the same numbers can be used to make one or two subtraction problems.

RULE: For every addition problem, the same numbers can be used to make one or two subtraction problems.

NOTE: Show students the two ways a subtraction problem can be written:

$$16 - 7 = 9 \text{ or } \begin{array}{r} 16 \\ \underline{-7} \\ 9 \end{array}$$

Name ______________________________

ADDITION ASSESSMENT

1. 5 + 4 = ____
2. 3 + 1 = ____
3. 10 + 10 = ____
4. 2 + 0 = ____
5. 5 + 5 = ____
6. 3 + 3 = ____
7. 3 + 2 = ____
8. 6 + 6 = ____
9. 0 + 0 = ____
10. 9 + 4 = ____
11. 1 + 2 = ____
12. 5 + 2 = ____
13. 4 + 0 = ____
14. 1 + 8 = ____
15. 8 + 8 = ____
16. 4 + 3 = ____
17. 9 + 1 = ____
18. 1 + 4 = ____
19. 6 + 3 = ____
20. 0 + 1 = ____
21. 10 + 4 = ____
22. 6 + 5 = ____
23. 0 + 3 = ____
24. 7 + 7 = ____
25. 9 + 8 = ____
26. 8 + 7 = ____
27. 1 + 1 = ____
28. 3 + 7 = ____
29. 5 + 1 = ____
30. 5 + 7 = ____
31. 10 + 3 = ____
32. 4 + 4 = ____
33. 7 + 9 = ____
34. 0 + 5 = ____
35. 8 + 3 = ____
36. 4 + 6 = ____
37. 1 + 6 = ____
38. 6 + 0 = ____
39. 3 + 9 = ____
40. 2 + 6 = ____
41. 7 + 1 = ____
42. 9 + 2 = ____
43. 0 + 7 = ____
44. 2 + 2 = ____
45. 7 + 6 = ____
46. 10 + 8 = ____
47. 2 + 8 = ____
48. 8 + 5 = ____
49. 7 + 2 = ____
50. 7 + 4 = ____
51. 10 + 1 = ____
52. 8 + 0 = ____
53. 5 + 9 = ____
54. 9 + 6 = ____
55. 2 + 4 = ____
56. 0 + 9 = ____
57. 3 + 5 = ____
58. 10 + 5 = ____
59. 10 + 0 = ____
60. 10 + 9 = ____
61. 6 + 8 = ____
62. 4 + 8 = ____
63. 10 + 7 = ____
64. 10 + 6 = ____
65. 10 + 2 = ____
66. 9 + 9 = ____

Name ______________________________ **WORKSHEET B**

SUBTRACTION

Answer each addition problem. Make two subtraction problems from the same numbers.

1. 3	7	7	2. 2	[ ]	[ ]	3. 5	[ ]	[ ]
+4	-3	-4	+4	-2	-4	+6	-5	-6
7	4	3	[ ]			[ ]		
4. 8	[ ]	[ ]	5. 3	[ ]	[ ]	6. 4	[ ]	[ ]
+2	-8	-2	+6	-3	-6	+1	-4	-1
[ ]			[ ]			[ ]		
7. 3	[ ]	[ ]	8. 2	[ ]	[ ]	9. 4	[ ]	[ ]
+9	-3	-9	+7	-2	-7	+7	-4	-7
[ ]			[ ]			[ ]		
10. 4	[ ]	[ ]	11. 8	[ ]	[ ]	12. 7	[ ]	[ ]
+5	-4	-5	+3	-8	-3	+8	-7	-8
[ ]			[ ]			[ ]		

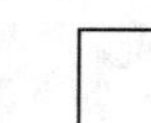

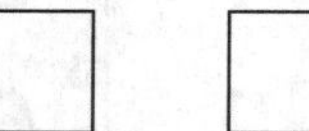

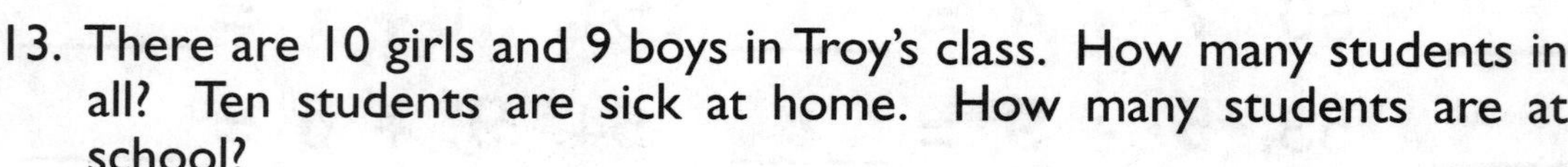

13. There are 10 girls and 9 boys in Troy's class. How many students in all? Ten students are sick at home. How many students are at school?

CHALLENGE:

a. 33	[ ]		b. 27	[ ]		c. 66	[ ]		d. 55	[ ]
+44	-33		+72	-27		+33	-33		+22	-22
[ ]	[ ]		[ ]	[ ]		[ ]	[ ]		[ ]	[ ]

Name ______________________________ **WORKSHEET C**

SUBTRACTION

Answer each addition problem. Make two subtraction problems from the same numbers.

1. 4	☐	☐	2. 3	☐	☐	3. 6	☐	☐
<u>+7</u>	<u>-4</u>	<u>-7</u>	<u>+5</u>	<u>-3</u>	<u>-5</u>	<u>+4</u>	<u>-6</u>	<u>-4</u>
☐			☐			☐		
4. 3	☐	☐	5. 2	☐	☐	6. 7	☐	☐
<u>+7</u>	<u>-3</u>	<u>-7</u>	<u>+9</u>	<u>-2</u>	<u>-9</u>	<u>+6</u>	<u>-7</u>	<u>-6</u>
☐			☐			☐		
7. 8	☐	☐	8. 9	☐	☐	9. 7	☐	☐
<u>+4</u>	<u>-8</u>	<u>-4</u>	<u>+8</u>	<u>-9</u>	<u>-8</u>	<u>+5</u>	<u>-7</u>	<u>-5</u>
☐			☐			☐		
10. 9	☐	☐	11. 6	☐	☐	12. 7	☐	☐
<u>+4</u>	<u>-9</u>	<u>-4</u>	<u>+9</u>	<u>-6</u>	<u>-9</u>	<u>+9</u>	<u>-7</u>	<u>-9</u>
☐			☐			☐		

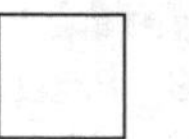
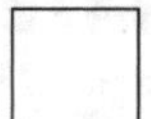
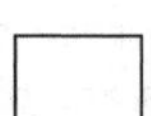

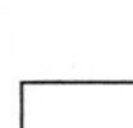

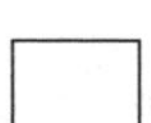

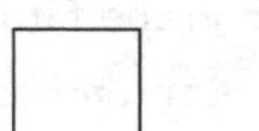
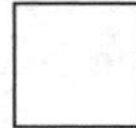

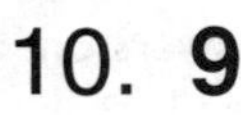
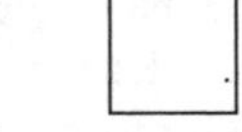
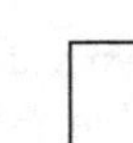

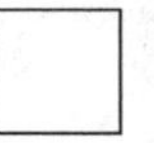
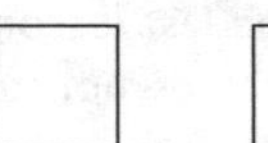

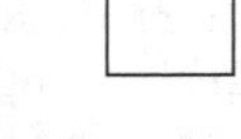

13. Gretchen has 17 dollars. She spent 8 dollars. How much change should she get?

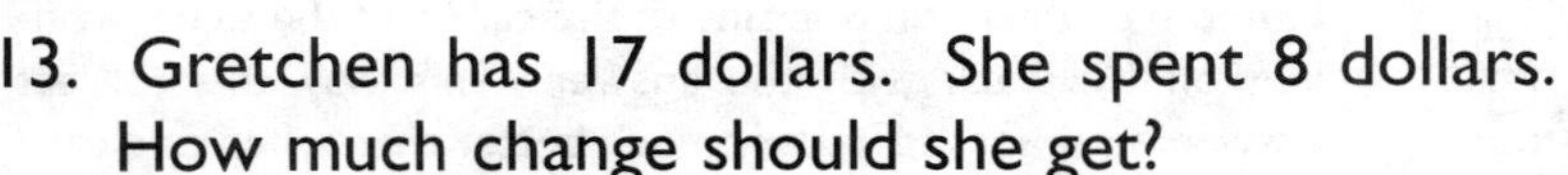

14. She has 15 minutes to shop. She was in the toy shop for 6 minutes. How much time does she have left?

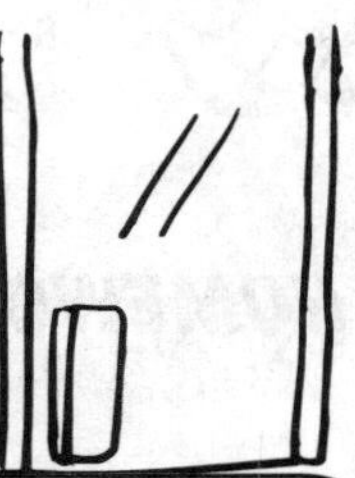

CHALLENGE:

Gretchen's mother bought 3 packs of soda with 6 cans in each pack. They drank 4 cans. How many cans are left?

LESSON PLAN 3

OBJECTIVE: Addition doubles as subtraction problems. Students will learn the subtraction facts which are made from the addition doubles.

MATERIALS: Number Line (page 13), Flash Cards (pages 21-28); Practice Facts for Doubles (page 29); Travel Folder for Doubles (pages 30); students could make their own on index cards; Worksheet D (page 31); progress charts (pages 32 and 33)

DEMONSTRATION OF EVENS AND ODDS: Have eight students stand up. Tell them they are to form two teams for recess. Count them off into two teams. If the two teams are the same size, eight is an even number. There are two teams of four, so write 8 on the board under the word *even*. Now have seven students stand up. They cannot be divided into two same-size teams. Write 7 on the board under the word *odd*. Do the same with several other numbers. Circle the even numbers on a number line. Ask students to guess which other numbers are even. If they can't see the pattern, do a few more. What they need to remember in the future is:

RULE: An even number is any number which ends in 0, 2, 4, 6 or 8. An odd number is any number which ends in 1, 3, 5, 7 or 9.

SUBTRACTION: Now have students give you the subtraction problem which can be made from each of the doubles problems listed in the Introduction. If they understood the last lesson, this should be easy. If not, use a number line to demonstrate that:

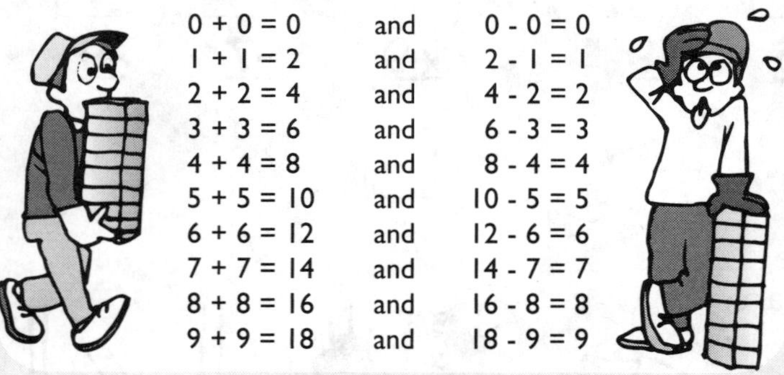

0 + 0 = 0	and	0 - 0 = 0
1 + 1 = 2	and	2 - 1 = 1
2 + 2 = 4	and	4 - 2 = 2
3 + 3 = 6	and	6 - 3 = 3
4 + 4 = 8	and	8 - 4 = 4
5 + 5 = 10	and	10 - 5 = 5
6 + 6 = 12	and	12 - 6 = 6
7 + 7 = 14	and	14 - 7 = 7
8 + 8 = 16	and	16 - 8 = 8
9 + 9 = 18	and	18 - 9 = 9

HOMEWORK: Worksheet D.

PROGRESS CHART: Send home the Student's Math Phonics™ Progress Chart so that a parent can sign a space when the student has learned them.

INTRODUCTION: Addition doubles are problems in which the two numbers being added are the same. Have the students give the doubles and write them on the board.

0 + 0 = 0 1 + 1 = 2 2 + 2 = 4 3 + 3 = 6 4 + 4 = 8

5 + 5 = 10 6 + 6 = 12 7 + 7 = 14 8 + 8 = 16 9 + 9 = 18

Point out to the class that the answers are all even numbers–like counting by 2. If you did not use *Math Phonics™–Addition*, take a few minutes to demonstrate even and odd numbers. Most students will learn this concept very easily, but it is much easier to remember a new idea if it is demonstrated.

TAKE-HOME: Send home the Travel Folder for Doubles. Show students how to fold it from left to right so that only one column shows at a time. Column one is used for practice. Column two is a compound flash card. Students read the problem and give the correct answer from memory. They can turn back to column one to see if they are right.

Students should discuss with their parents where would be a good place to post the folder at home.

Tell the students to bring the travel folder in the car with them and practice while their parents are driving. (This is why it is called a travel folder.) Also, another good time to get help from a parent would be while supper is being prepared.

OPTIONAL: Enlarge and laminate the Travel Folder for Doubles in subtraction and post it in the classroom so students can drill the facts when they have free time.

ASSIGNMENT: Have students fill in the answers on the Practice Facts for Doubles sheet. Use number lines if necessary. This is a study sheet, so you can do this as a class if you like.

FLASH CARDS: Copy the subtraction flash cards in this book for each student, or have each student make a set using index cards. If the students make their own, be sure to have the problem on one side of the card and the same problem on the back with the answer. This way, the correct answer is reinforced visually much better than when one card has two different facts on the two sides with the answer in tiny print in the corner.

GAMES: Flash cards can be used in place of the question cards in Trivial Pursuit™ or other board games. Roll dice and play according to the rules.

<table>
<tr><td>9
- 2</td><td>8
- 2</td><td>7
- 2</td><td>6
- 2</td><td>5
- 2</td><td>4
- 2</td><td>3
- 2</td></tr>
<tr><td>2
- 2</td><td>10
- 1</td><td>9
- 1</td><td>8
- 1</td><td>7
- 1</td><td>6
- 1</td><td>5
- 1</td></tr>
<tr><td>4
- 1</td><td>3
- 1</td><td>2
- 1</td><td>1
- 1</td><td>9
- 0</td><td>8
- 0</td><td>7
- 0</td></tr>
<tr><td>6
- 0</td><td>5
- 0</td><td>4
- 0</td><td>3
- 0</td><td>2
- 0</td><td>1
- 0</td><td>0
- 0</td></tr>
</table>

$\begin{array}{r}3\\-2\\\hline 1\end{array}$	$\begin{array}{r}4\\-2\\\hline 2\end{array}$	$\begin{array}{r}5\\-2\\\hline 3\end{array}$	$\begin{array}{r}6\\-2\\\hline 4\end{array}$	$\begin{array}{r}7\\-2\\\hline 5\end{array}$	$\begin{array}{r}8\\-2\\\hline 6\end{array}$	$\begin{array}{r}9\\-2\\\hline 7\end{array}$
$\begin{array}{r}5\\-1\\\hline 4\end{array}$	$\begin{array}{r}6\\-1\\\hline 5\end{array}$	$\begin{array}{r}7\\-1\\\hline 6\end{array}$	$\begin{array}{r}8\\-1\\\hline 7\end{array}$	$\begin{array}{r}9\\-1\\\hline 8\end{array}$	$\begin{array}{r}10\\-1\\\hline 9\end{array}$	$\begin{array}{r}2\\-2\\\hline 0\end{array}$
$\begin{array}{r}7\\-0\\\hline 7\end{array}$	$\begin{array}{r}8\\-0\\\hline 8\end{array}$	$\begin{array}{r}9\\-0\\\hline 9\end{array}$	$\begin{array}{r}1\\-1\\\hline 0\end{array}$	$\begin{array}{r}2\\-1\\\hline 1\end{array}$	$\begin{array}{r}3\\-1\\\hline 2\end{array}$	$\begin{array}{r}4\\-1\\\hline 3\end{array}$
$\begin{array}{r}0\\-0\\\hline 0\end{array}$	$\begin{array}{r}1\\-0\\\hline 1\end{array}$	$\begin{array}{r}2\\-0\\\hline 2\end{array}$	$\begin{array}{r}3\\-0\\\hline 3\end{array}$	$\begin{array}{r}4\\-0\\\hline 4\end{array}$	$\begin{array}{r}5\\-0\\\hline 5\end{array}$	$\begin{array}{r}6\\-0\\\hline 6\end{array}$

7 - 7	10 - 6	9 - 6	8 - 6	7 - 6	6 - 6	10 - 5
9 - 5	8 - 5	7 - 5	6 - 5	5 - 5	10 - 4	9 - 4
8 - 4	7 - 4	6 - 4	5 - 4	4 - 4	10 - 3	9 - 3
8 - 3	7 - 3	6 - 3	5 - 3	4 - 3	3 - 3	10 - 2

$\begin{array}{r}7\\-7\\\hline 0\end{array}$	$\begin{array}{r}9\\-5\\\hline 4\end{array}$	$\begin{array}{r}8\\-4\\\hline 4\end{array}$	$\begin{array}{r}8\\-3\\\hline 5\end{array}$
$\begin{array}{r}10\\-6\\\hline 4\end{array}$	$\begin{array}{r}8\\-5\\\hline 3\end{array}$	$\begin{array}{r}7\\-4\\\hline 3\end{array}$	$\begin{array}{r}7\\-3\\\hline 4\end{array}$
$\begin{array}{r}9\\-6\\\hline 3\end{array}$	$\begin{array}{r}7\\-5\\\hline 2\end{array}$	$\begin{array}{r}6\\-4\\\hline 2\end{array}$	$\begin{array}{r}6\\-3\\\hline 3\end{array}$
$\begin{array}{r}8\\-6\\\hline 2\end{array}$	$\begin{array}{r}6\\-5\\\hline 1\end{array}$	$\begin{array}{r}5\\-4\\\hline 1\end{array}$	$\begin{array}{r}5\\-3\\\hline 2\end{array}$
$\begin{array}{r}7\\-6\\\hline 1\end{array}$	$\begin{array}{r}5\\-5\\\hline 0\end{array}$	$\begin{array}{r}4\\-4\\\hline 0\end{array}$	$\begin{array}{r}4\\-3\\\hline 1\end{array}$
$\begin{array}{r}6\\-6\\\hline 0\end{array}$	$\begin{array}{r}10\\-4\\\hline 6\end{array}$	$\begin{array}{r}10\\-3\\\hline 7\end{array}$	$\begin{array}{r}3\\-3\\\hline 0\end{array}$
$\begin{array}{r}10\\-5\\\hline 5\end{array}$	$\begin{array}{r}9\\-4\\\hline 5\end{array}$	$\begin{array}{r}9\\-3\\\hline 6\end{array}$	$\begin{array}{r}10\\-2\\\hline 8\end{array}$

13 - 6	13 - 7	13 - 8	13 - 9	14 - 5	14 - 6	14 - 7
14 - 8	14 - 9	15 - 6	15 - 7	15 - 8	15 - 9	16 - 7
16 - 8	16 - 9	17 - 8	17 - 9	18 - 9	10 - 10	10 - 9
9 - 9	10 - 8	9 - 8	8 - 8	10 - 7	9 - 7	8 - 7

14 - 7 7	14 - 6 8	14 - 5 9	13 - 9 4	13 - 8 5	13 - 7 6	13 - 6 7
16 - 7 9	15 - 9 6	15 - 8 7	15 - 7 8	15 - 6 9	14 - 9 5	14 - 8 6
10 - 9 1	10 -10 0	18 - 9 9	17 - 9 8	17 - 8 9	16 - 9 7	16 - 8 8
8 - 7 1	9 - 7 2	10 - 7 3	8 - 8 0	9 - 8 1	10 - 8 2	9 - 9 0

				11 - 2	11 - 3	11 - 4
11 - 5	11 - 6	11 - 7	11 - 8	11 - 9	12 - 3	12 - 4
12 - 5	12 - 6	12 - 7	12 - 8	12 - 9	13 - 4	13 - 5

		11 -5 6	12 -5 7
		11 -6 5	12 -6 6
		11 -7 4	12 -7 5
		11 -8 3	12 -8 4
	11 -2 9	11 -9 2	12 -9 3
	11 -3 8	12 -3 9	13 -4 9
	11 -4 7	12 -4 8	13 -5 8

Name ______________________________

PRACTICE FACTS FOR DOUBLES

Addition	Subtraction
0 + 0 = ____	____ - 0 = 0
1 + 1 = ____	____ - 1 = 1
2 + 2 = ____	____ - 2 = 2
3 + 3 = ____	____ - 3 = 3
4 + 4 = ____	____ - 4 = 4
5 + 5 = ____	____ - 5 = 5
6 + 6 = ____	____ - 6 = 6
7 + 7 = ____	____ - 7 = 7
8 + 8 = ____	____ - 8 = 8
9 + 9 = ____	____ - 9 = 9

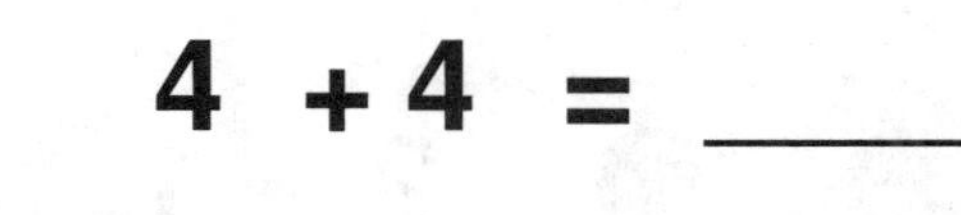

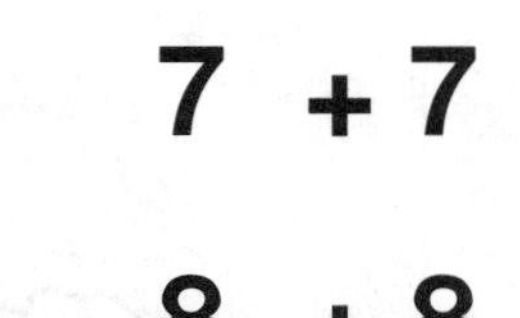

For addition doubles, answers are even numbers.

Name ________________________________

TRAVEL FOLDER FOR DOUBLES

18 - 9 = 9	●	●	18 - 9
16 - 8 = 8	●	●	16 - 8
14 - 7 = 7	●	●	14 - 7
12 - 6 = 6	●	●	12 - 6
10 - 5 = 5	●	●	10 - 5
8 - 4 = 4	●	●	8 - 4
6 - 3 = 3	●	●	6 - 3
4 - 2 = 2	●	●	4 - 2
2 - 1 = 1	●	●	2 - 1
0 - 0 = 0	●	●	0 - 0

ame ______________________________

DOUBLES

Circle these words in the puzzle on the right:

addition	multiplication	sum
division	numbers	zero
factor	subtraction	

R	N	B	S	T	O	N	A	X	E	S	T	Z	L
A	B	X	U	S	T	O	D	A	R	N	P	E	S
S	T	U	B	A	L	T	D	O	L	N	I	R	T
M	U	L	T	I	P	L	I	C	A	T	I	O	N
Q	O	N	R	T	L	B	T	S	N	X	Z	Y	T
T	O	N	A	R	P	D	I	V	I	S	I	O	N
S	U	P	C	L	Y	S	O	E	N	U	T	R	Y
F	A	C	T	O	R	Q	N	R	P	M	S	T	O
D	Y	S	I	N	M	U	S	T	X	M	L	P	Z
A	E	I	O	U	N	I	L	U	S	T	E	R	Y
P	O	N	N	U	M	B	E	R	S	C	R	G	Y

Learn to say and spell these words:

add-i-tion	num-bers
di-vi-sion	sub-trac-tion
fac-tor	sum
mul-ti-pli-ca-tion	ze-ro

Circle the even numbers.

1 2 3 4 5 6 7 8 9 10 11 12 13 14 15 16 17

23 29 24 26 32 35 34 38 66 56 67 87 88 68 69

Subtract.

1. **10 - 5 =** ______ 2. **12 - 6 =** ______ 3. **4 - 2 =** ______

4. **6 - 3 =** ______ 5. **16 - 8 =** ______ 6. **2 - 1 =** ______

7. **14 - 7 =** ______ 8. **8 - 4 =** ______ 9. **18 - 9 =** ______

10. Five sets of twins got on the bus. How many kids got on the bus?
11. One set of twins got off the bus. How many twins are still on the bus?
12. Each of the twins is wearing gloves. How many gloves are on the bus now?

CHALLENGE:

What is the total number of fingers and thumbs on all those gloves?

Name ______________________________

STUDENT'S MATH PHONICS™ PROGRESS CHART

	Say Facts in Order	Not in Order	Worksheet Scores	
Doubles			D	
Number Neighbors			E	F (Review)
1s				
0s			G	H (Review)
0s/Matching Facts				
9s			J	K (Review)
9s/Matching Facts				
2s			L	M
2s/Matching Facts				
Number Pairs for 7, 8 and 9			O	P
Number Pairs for 10 and 11			Q	R
Last 12 Facts			S	T (Review)
Bingo 100			U	V
Assessment				

Have parent or teacher sign each space when you can say the facts (first two columns).

TEACHER'S MATH PHONICS™ PROGRESS CHART

Name	Doubles	Number Neighbors	1s	0s and M.F.	9s and M.F.	2s and M.F.	Number Pairs for 7, 8 and 9	Number Pairs for 10 and 11	Number Pairs for 12, 13, 14 and 15	Assessment First Time	Assessment Second Try

t a check mark or date as groups are learned.

LESSON PLAN 4

OBJECTIVE: Students will learn to subtract number neighbors and also the "matching facts" in which one is subtracted from a number.

MATERIALS: Number Line (page 13), Flash Cards (pages 21-28), Practice Facts for Number Neighbors and 1s (page 35), Travel Folder for Number Neighbors and Subtracting 1 (page 36), Worksheets E and F (pages 37 and 38)

INTRODUCTION: Have the class as a whole recite the first column from the Travel Folder for Doubles (page 30).

If you taught addition using the *Math Phonics*™ book, students are familiar with number neighbors. If not, explain that number neighbors are two numbers side-by-side on the number line. 5 and 6 are number neighbors–6 and 7 are also number neighbors. Have the class name several other number neighbor pairs. Using the number line, find the answer to the subtraction problems. For example:

10 - 9 = 1	7 - 6 = 1	4 - 3 = 1
9 - 8 = 1	6 - 5 = 1	3 - 2 = 1
8 - 7 = 1	5 - 4 = 1	2 - 1 = 1

RULE: When you subtract number neighbors, the answer is always one.

TAKE-HOME: Worksheets E and F.

MATCHING FACTS: In subtraction, we can make another problem with the same three numbers. We call these problems the matching facts. Here are some examples:

10 - 1 = 9	5 - 1 = 4
9 - 1 = 8	4 - 1 = 3
8 - 1 = 7	3 - 1 = 2
7 - 1 = 6	2 - 1 = 1
6 - 1 = 5	

Subtracting one seems simple, but I have observed some students who have had a lot of trouble with it. Subtracting one is easy if students think of the smaller number neighbor.

RULE: When you subtract one from a number, the answer is the smaller number neighbor.

ASSIGNMENT: Use Practice Facts sheets, Travel Folders and flash cards as described in Lesson Plan 3 (page 20).

QUIZ BOWL: Start using the subtraction flash cards to play Quiz Bowl when you have a few minutes at the end of a class period. Follow the rules on page 39.

DOMINO FLASH CARDS: Use a standard set of dominoes. This can be a one- or two-player game. Turn all dominoes facedown. Turn over one domino. Count the spots on each end. Make a subtraction problem–larger number minus smaller number. Give the answer. If students cannot think of the answer, they can use the spots to help count out the answer.

For a two-player game, students take turns turning over a domino. If they give the correct answer, they keep the domino. If they miss, they return it to the pile. The one with the most dominoes at the end wins. Use the subtraction facts page to check answers.

OPTIONAL: Use the eight math words in the word find on Worksheet D (page 31) as a spelling test. Tell the students ahead of time so they can study. Help them learn the long words by sounding out each syllable. Have them write the words on the back of Worksheet E (page 37).

Name ____________________

PRACTICE FACTS FOR NUMBER NEIGHBORS AND 1s

10 - 9 = ________

9 - 8 = ________

8 - 7 = ________

7 - 6 = ________

6 - 5 = ________

5 - 4 = ________

4 - 3 = ________

3 - 2 = ________

2 - 1 = ________

10 - 1 = ________

9 - 1 = ________

8 - 1 = ________

7 - 1 = ________

6 - 1 = ________

5 - 1 = ________

4 - 1 = ________

3 - 1 = ________

2 - 1 = ________

When you subtract number neighbors, the answer is one.

Name ________________________________

TRAVEL FOLDER FOR NUMBER NEIGHBORS AND SUBTRACTING 1

10 - 9 = 1	10 - 9	10 - 1 = 9	10 - 1
9 - 8 = 1	9 - 8	9 - 1 = 8	9 - 1
8 - 7 = 1	8 - 7	8 - 1 = 7	8 - 1
7 - 6 = 1	7 - 6	7 - 1 = 6	7 - 1
6 - 5 = 1	6 - 5	6 - 1 = 5	6 - 1
5 - 4 = 1	5 - 4	5 - 1 = 4	5 - 1
4 - 3 = 1	4 - 3	4 - 1 = 3	4 - 1
3 - 2 = 1	3 - 2	3 - 1 = 2	3 - 1
2 - 1 = 1	2 - 1	2 - 1 = 1	2 - 1

Name ______________________________

NUMBER NEIGHBORS AND 1s

Put an X above each number neighbor problem. Do all problems.

1.	2.	3.	4.	5.
3 − 2	10 − 1	6 − 1	2 − 1	8 − 1

6.	7.	8.	9.	10.
8 − 7	5 − 1	4 − 3	10 − 9	4 − 1

11.	12.	13.	14.	15.
9 − 1	5 − 4	7 − 1	8 − 1	6 − 5

16.	17.	18.	19.	20.
6 − 1	7 − 6	3 − 1	9 − 8	10 − 9

21. There were 10 pizzas at the class party. One is left over. How many pizzas were eaten?
22. Bill bought 9 packs of gum. He gave one pack to the teacher. How many packs are left?

CHALLENGE:
After giving one pack to the teacher, Bill took the other packs to his desk. There are 5 sticks of gum in each pack. Bill gave away 6 sticks. How many sticks of gum does Bill have left?

Name ______________________________

REVIEW

Put an X above each number neighbor problem. Do all problems.

1. 8 − 7	2. 10 − 5	3. 10 − 9	4. 2 − 1	5. 10 − 1
6. 12 − 6	7. 6 − 1	8. 4 − 2	9. 9 − 8	10. 14 − 7
11. 7 − 6	12. 6 − 3	13. 6 − 5	14. 16 − 8	15. 9 − 1
16. 8 − 4	17. 4 − 1	18. 18 − 9	19. 8 − 1	20. 5 − 4
21. 5 − 1	22. 20 − 10	23. 3 − 2	24. 7 − 1	25. 4 − 3

26. Adam saw 14 cars in the school yard. Seven cars are red. How many cars are not red?

CHALLENGE:
Six cars drove away. Nine more drove in. Five more left. How many cars are in the school yard now?

QUIZ BOWL

Set aside 5 or 10 minutes at the end of each day for a classroom quiz bowl.

1. Divide the class into two teams.

2. Use math flash cards for questions.

3. Keep index cards at hand. When the quicker students finish their work early, have them write a question from another subject on an index card.* Check to be sure that they are appropriate. Use these as well as the flash cards.

4. Keep track of points. Give a small prize at the end of the week–perhaps gum or a pencil for each member of the winning team. A free homework pass is a good prize, but don't use that very often. Parents could be asked to donate prizes.

*Other students could take index cards home to write questions. Have students put names on cards and thank them for the question when it is used.

LESSON PLAN 5

OBJECTIVE: Students will learn subtracting zero and subtracting a number from itself.

MATERIALS: Flash Cards (page 21-28); Number Line (page 13); Worksheets G, H and I (pages 41-44)

INTRODUCTION: Have the class chant the subtraction facts for number neighbors and subtracting one. They should also chant the doubles subtraction problems until everyone knows them. Preview previous rules.

REVIEW: Ask the class for the answers to the addition problems involving zero:

0 + 0 = 0	4 + 0 = 4	8 + 0 = 8
1 + 0 = 1	5 + 0 = 5	9 + 0 = 9
2 + 0 = 2	6 + 0 = 6	10 + 0 = 10
3 + 0 = 3	7 + 0 = 7	

When we make subtraction problems with these addition facts, we find:

0 - 0 = 0	4 - 0 = 4	8 - 0 = 8
1 - 0 = 1	5 - 0 = 5	9 - 0 = 9
2 - 0 = 2	6 - 0 = 6	10 - 0 = 10
3 - 0 = 3	7 - 0 = 7	

Matching facts are:

0 - 0 = 0	4 - 4 = 0	8 - 8 = 0
1 - 1 = 0	5 - 5 = 0	9 - 9 = 0
2 - 2 = 0	6 - 6 = 0	10 - 10 = 0
3 - 3 = 0	7 - 7 = 0	

Use a number line if necessary.

This should be easy for students to understand. It is not necessary to use practice facts sheets and travel folders for these groups. We will just go to worksheets, and they will combine the 0s, number neighbors, 1s and doubles.

FLASH CARDS: Have students cut out or make flash cards for these facts and add to the number neighbors, 1s and doubles they have been studying.

SUBTRACTION BINGO: Follow the rules on page 50 and use the grids on page 51. Do not use large amounts of time in class for games. You can play a game in just minutes at the end of class. Also, students can play the game at home for practice.

Name ______________________________

Os AND MATCHING FACTS

Put an X above each number neighbor problem. Do all problems.

1. 3 − 0	2. 10 − 10	3. 10 − 0	4. 6 − 6	5. 5 − 0
6. 5 − 5	7. 9 − 0	8. 9 − 9	9. 4 − 0	10. 4 − 4
11. 8 − 0	12. 8 − 8	13. 3 − 3	14. 7 − 0	15. 2 − 2
16. 7 − 7	17. 2 − 0	18. 6 − 0	19. 1 − 1	20. 1 − 0

Find each answer. Then put each letter in the space below with the same number.

How do cows do their shopping?

6 − 3 = 3	6 − 0	7 − 0	5 − 4	9 − 1	10 − 5	8 − 4	3 − 1
(A)	(C)	(Y)	(L)	(B)	(T)	(O)	(G)

___ ___   ___ A ___ A ___ ___ ___

8 7   6 3 5 3 1 4 2

Name ______________________

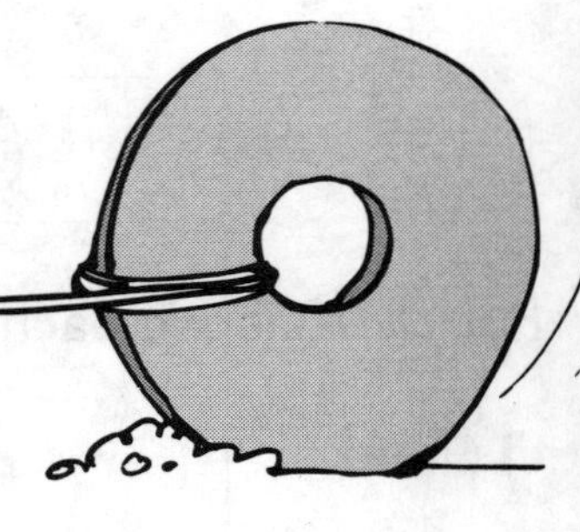

REVIEW

1. 6 - 6	2. 10 - 9	3. 9 - 1	4. 10 - 5	5. 6 - 1
6. 3 - 1	7. 10 - 10	8. 9 - 0	9. 18 - 9	10. 8 - 7
11. 16 - 8	12. 8 - 0	13. 14 - 7	14. 10 - 0	15. 7 - 1
16. 7 - 0	17. 12 - 6	18. 5 - 0	19. 8 - 4	20. 4 - 0
21. 6 - 0	22. 6 - 3	23. 4 - 2	24. 4 - 4	25. 2 - 1
26. 4 - 1	27. 9 - 8	28. 7 - 7	29. 6 - 5	30. 5 - 1

Name ______________________

REVIEW

31. 3 - 3	32. 3 - 0	33. 1 - 1	34. 1 - 0	35. 9 - 9
36. 8 - 8	37. 10 - 1	38. 2 - 0	39. 5 - 5	40. 2 - 2
41. 7 - 6	42. 8 - 4	43. 2 - 1	44. 8 - 1	45. 3 - 2
46. 5 - 4	47. 10 - 0	48. 4 - 3	49. 9 - 9	50. 8 - 7

51. J'Cora and Ann are frosting cookies. They started with 16. They have frosted 8. How many cookies are left?

52. Of the 16 cookies, they gave away 1 and took the rest to school. How many cookies did they take to school?

CHALLENGE:
Three other people also brought cookies. Each of them brought 12. Counting J'Cora's and Ann's cookies, how many were brought to school?

Name ______________________________

DYNAMITE COLORS

Choose two colors.

Color 1: __________ if the answer is 0 or 1.

Color 2: __________ for all other answers.

7 - 6 = _____

4 + 4 = _____

3 + 3 = _____

5 - 5 = _____

7 + 7 = _____

9 + 9 = _____

8 - 8 = _____

6 - 0 = _____

8 - 1 = _____

LESSON PLAN 6

OBJECTIVE: 9s and matching facts. Students will be taught a pattern to help in learning the 9s. They will also learn the matching facts in which the answer is nine.

MATERIALS: Number Lines, if necessary (page 13), Practice Facts for 9s (page 46), Travel Folder for 9s (page 47), Worksheets J and K (pages 48 and 49)

INTRODUCTION: The class should chant the subtraction facts for doubles if necessary. Also, do subtracting one and subtracting number neighbors as chants. Review rules.

The chants for subtracting zero and subtracting a number from itself are so simple, you may only need to do them once. There is nothing to be gained from boring the students with things too simple.

ASSIGNMENT: Worksheets J and K.

DICE FLASH CARDS: Use two standard dice. Roll the dice. Make a subtraction problem. Give the answer. If two players are playing, give one point for each correct answer. The first player to get 20 points wins. Use the Subtraction Facts (page 9) to check for correct answers.

REVIEW: Ask the class for the addition facts for adding nine to a number. Put them on the board:

1 + 9 = 10	2 + 9 = 11	3 + 9 = 12
4 + 9 = 13	5 + 9 = 14	6 + 9 = 15
7 + 9 = 16	8 + 9 = 17	9 + 9 = 18

Ask students for the subtraction facts made from these problems:

10 - 9 = 1	11 - 9 = 2	12 - 9 = 3
13 - 9 = 4	14 - 9 = 5	15 - 9 = 6
16 - 9 = 7	17 - 9 = 8	18 - 9 = 9

Pass out practice facts sheets and number lines. Have students check that these answers are correct.

Ask the class if they see any pattern here. You want them to see that they could get the answer by adding the two numbers they started with. For example: 14 - 9 = 5. They started with 14: 1 + 4 = 5. 15 - 9 = 6. They started with 15: 1 + 5 = 6.

RULE: When subtracting nine from a number in the teens, add the two numerals of the teens number. That is the answer.

Now ask students for the matching facts for those subtraction problems.

10 - 1 = 9	11 - 2 = 9	12 - 3 = 9
13 - 4 = 9	14 - 5 = 9	15 - 6 = 9
16 - 7 = 9	17 - 8 = 9	18 - 9 = 9

Have students fill out the practice facts sheet using a number line to be sure these are the correct answers. Point out to the students that for the 9s, the numbers in the 1s column are number neighbors. When you try to subtract the larger number neighbor from the smaller number neighbor, the answer is nine.

RULE: When you subtract a one-digit number from a number in the teens and you are taking a smaller number neighbor minus a larger number neighbor, the answer is nine.

Name ______________________________

PRACTICE FACTS FOR 9s

10 - 9 = ______	10 - 1 = ______
11 - 9 = ______	11 - 2 = ______
12 - 9 = ______	12 - 3 = ______
13 - 9 = ______	13 - 4 = ______
14 - 9 = ______	14 - 5 = ______
15 - 9 = ______	15 - 6 = ______
16 - 9 = ______	16 - 7 = ______
17 - 9 = ______	17 - 8 = ______
18 - 9 = ______	18 - 9 = ______

Name ______________________________

TRAVEL FOLDER FOR 9s

10 - 9 = 1	10 - 9	10 - 1 = 9	10 - 1
11 - 9 = 2	11 - 9	11 - 2 = 9	11 - 2
12 - 9 = 3	12 - 9	12 - 3 = 9	12 - 3
13 - 9 = 4	13 - 9	13 - 4 = 9	13 - 4
14 - 9 = 5	14 - 9	14 - 5 = 9	14 - 5
15 - 9 = 6	15 - 9	15 - 6 = 9	15 - 6
16 - 9 = 7	16 - 9	16 - 7 = 9	16 - 7
17 - 9 = 8	17 - 9	17 - 8 = 9	17 - 8
18 - 9 = 9	18 - 9	18 - 9 = 9	18 - 9

Name ______________________________

9s AND MATCHING FACTS

1.	2.	3.	4.	5.
14 - 5	10 - 9	15 - 6	14 - 9	10 - 1

6.	7.	8.	9.	10.
16 - 9	16 - 7	11 - 9	11 - 2	15 - 9

11.	12.	13.	14.	15.
17 - 8	17 - 9	12 - 3	12 - 9	18 - 9

16.	17.	18.	19.	20.
16 - 7	13 - 4	18 - 9	11 - 2	13 - 9

21. Luis and Dan have 17 action figures in all. Eight are broken. How many figures are not broken?
22. Nine of the 17 figures have moving parts. How many figures do not have moving parts?

CHALLENGE:
On the way home, the boys lost 5 of their 17 figures. They also bought 10 new ones. Now how many do they have in all?

Name ____________________

REVIEW

1.	2.	3.	4.	5.
3 - 2	2 - 1	15 - 9	12 - 3	10 - 9

6.	7.	8.	9.	10.
4 - 2	16 - 9	13 - 4	11 - 9	6 - 3

11.	12.	13.	14.	15.
17 - 9	14 - 5	12 - 9	8 - 4	4 - 3

16.	17.	18.	19.	20.
15 - 6	13 - 9	10 - 5	5 - 4	16 - 8

21.	22.	23.	24.	25.
14 - 9	12 - 6	6 - 5	10 - 10	9 - 8

26.	27.	28.	29.	30.
14 - 7	7 - 8	10 - 9	17 - 8	18 - 9

SUBTRACTION BINGO

CLASSROOM GAME FOR PRACTICING SUBTRACTION FACTS

1. Use the flash cards for all the facts students are to have learned up to now. Add other cards as they are learned.

2. Give each student one 4" x 4" (10 x 10 cm) bingo grid. Cards can be laminated and reused or tossed.

3. Each student may choose one free space and write in the word *free*.

4. Numbers can be crossed out with a crayon over the laminated cards and rubbed clean with a facial tissue.

5. Write the flash card answers on the board.

6. Students write one answer in each square. It's OK if they can't use every number.

7. Call out a problem. Have the class say the answer as a group. Students cover the answer if they have it on their card. (Later you could call out the problem and not say the answer. Each student should think of the answer on his own.)

8. First to get four in a row wins. Give inexpensive school supplies as prizes–for example, a colorful pencil or eraser, a ruler with math facts, etc.

SUBTRACTION BINGO

LESSON PLAN 7

OBJECTIVE: 2s and matching facts. Students will be taught to subtract two from a number and will be taught the matching facts.

INTRODUCTION: Chant the subtraction facts for subtracting 9 and also the matching facts. Chant other groups until students have mastered them. Review rules.

CLASSROOM GAME: Ask someone in the class to give the even numbers from 2 to 20. Write them on the board. Do the same with the odd numbers from 1 to 19. You will call out an even number like 8 and point to a student. They will name the next smaller even number. Give some examples so students know what you mean. When a student gives a correct answer, they stand up. When all the class is standing, have them all sit and do the same with the odd numbers. This drill will help them learn to quickly subtract two from a number.

ASSIGNMENT: Worksheets L, M and N.

T-TABLES: For a quick worksheet, or quiz, have the students make a t-table like this:

-	2
11	
10	
9	
8	
7	
6	
5	
4	
3	
2	

The numbers in the left-hand column can also be jumbled.

NOTE: For the Challenge on page 55, demonstrate to the class that whenever you add an even number plus an odd number, the answer is odd.

MATERIALS: Flash Cards (pages 21-28); Practice Facts for 2s (page 53); Travel Folder for 2s (page 54); Worksheets L, M and N (pages 55-57)

REVIEW: Ask the class for the addition facts for adding 2 to a number. In the *Math Phonics™–Addition* book, they were arranged in two columns:

1 + 2 = 3	2 + 2 = 4
3 + 2 = 5	4 + 2 = 6
5 + 2 = 7	6 + 2 = 8
7 + 2 = 9	8 + 2 = 10
9 + 2 = 11	

This is to show that adding two to an odd number gives the next odd number and adding two to an even number gives the next even number.

Now write the subtraction problems for subtracting two in the same way. Use a number line to show that these are correct.

11 - 2 = 9	10 - 2 = 8
9 - 2 = 7	8 - 2 = 6
7 - 2 = 5	6 - 2 = 4
5 - 2 = 3	4 - 2 = 2
3 - 2 = 1	

Ask the class what pattern they see.

RULE: When you subtract two from an odd number, the answer is the next smaller odd number. When you subtract two from an even number, the answer is the next smaller even number.

Now look at the matching facts. Again, use a number line to demonstrate.

11 - 2 = 9	10 - 2 = 8
9 - 2 = 7	8 - 2 = 6
7 - 2 = 5	6 - 2 = 4
5 - 2 = 3	4 - 2 = 2
3 - 2 = 1	

These are odd numbers closest together on the number line and even numbers closest together on the number line. Ask students if they could make up a rule. This might be the rule:

RULE: When you subtract two closest odd numbers, the answer is two. When you subtract the two closest even numbers, the answer is two.

Have students fill out practice facts sheets using number lines if necessary. Hand out or have students make travel folders. Add flash cards to the ones being studied.

Name ______________________________

PRACTICE FACTS FOR 2s

11 - 2 = ____	11 - 9 = ____
9 - 2 = ____	9 - 7 = ____
7 - 2 = ____	7 - 5 = ____
5 - 2 = ____	5 - 3 = ____
3 - 2 = ____	3 - 1 = ____
12 - 2 = ____	12 - 10 = ____
10 - 2 = ____	10 - 8 = ____
8 - 2 = ____	8 - 6 = ____
6 - 2 = ____	6 - 4 = ____
4 - 2 = ____	4 - 2 = ____

To subtract two from an odd number, think of the next smaller odd number!

To subtract two from an even number, think of the next smaller even number!

Name ______________________________

TRAVEL FOLDER FOR 2s

12 - 2 = 10	12 - 2	12 - 10 = 2	12 - 10
11 - 2 = 9	11 - 2	11 - 9 = 2	11 - 9
10 - 2 = 8	10 - 2	10 - 8 = 2	10 - 8
9 - 2 = 7	9 - 2	9 - 7 = 2	9 - 7
8 - 2 = 6	8 - 2	8 - 6 = 2	8 - 6
7 - 2 = 5	7 - 2	7 - 5 = 2	7 - 5
6 - 2 = 4	6 - 2	6 - 4 = 2	6 - 4
5 - 2 = 3	5 - 2	5 - 3 = 2	5 - 3
4 - 2 = 2	4 - 2	4 - 2 = 2	4 - 2
3 - 2 = 1	3 - 2	3 - 1 = 2	3 - 1

Name ________________________________

2s AND MATCHING FACTS

1. 6 - 4	2. 12 - 2	3. 11 - 9	4. 11 - 2	5. 10 - 8
6. 7 - 6	7. 3 - 1	8. 10 - 2	9. 9 - 7	10. 6 - 2
11. 10 - 8	12. 9 - 2	13. 8 - 6	14. 5 - 2	15. 6 - 4
16. 8 - 2	17. 7 - 5	18. 4 - 2	19. 5 - 3	20. 3 - 2

21. Jake has a pack of 10 markers. Two markers are dried up. How many markers still work?

22. He buys another pack of 10. They all write. Now how many markers does he have that write?

CHALLENGE:
If Jake writes all of his even numbers in blue and all of his odd numbers in yellow, what color is an even number plus an odd number?

Name ______________________________

2s, 9s AND MATCHING FACTS

1. **4 - 2**	2. **7 - 5**	3. **10 - 1**	4. **10 - 2**	5. **17 - 8**
6. **18 - 9**	7. **3 - 2**	8. **10 - 8**	9. **9 - 2**	10. **11 - 2**
11. **17 - 9**	12. **9 - 7**	13. **8 - 2**	14. **12 - 3**	15. **17 - 8**
16. **8 - 6**	17. **7 - 2**	18. **13 - 4**	19. **6 - 4**	20. **14 - 5**
21. **13 - 4**	22. **6 - 2**	23. **5 - 3**	24. **15 - 6**	25. **3 - 1**
26. **5 - 2**	27. **14 - 5**	28. **15 - 6**	29. **16 - 7**	30. **16 - 9**

Name ______________________________ **WORKSHEET N**

A BLAST OF COLOR

Answer each problem. If the answer is 9, color that space purple; 8 = red; 7 = orange; 6 = yellow; 5 = green; 4 = blue.

10 - 1 = ___ 16 - 8 = ___ 14 - 7 = ___ 12 - 6 = ___ 10 - 5 = ___ 8 - 4 = ___

11 - 2 = ___

10 - 2 = ___

9 - 2 = ___

8 - 2 = ___

7 - 2 = ___

6 - 2 = ___

LESSON PLAN 8

OBJECTIVE: Number pairs for 7, 8 and 9. Students will be shown number pairs for seven, eight and nine, and learn the facts which have not already been taught.

INTRODUCTION: Chant the facts for subtracting two and their matching facts. Chant other groups as needed. Review rules.

MATERIALS: Subtraction Facts Chart (page 61); Practice Facts for Number Pairs for 7, 8 and 9 (page 63); Travel Folder for Number Pairs for 7 (page 64); Travel Folder for Number Pairs for 8 (page 65); Travel Folder for Number Pairs for 9 (page 66); Base 10 Counting Chart (page 67); Worksheets O and P (pages 68 and 69)

SUBTRACTION FACTS CHART: Look at the Subtraction Facts Chart on page 60. Groups that have been taught so far have been crossed off. 71 facts have been taught. 30 remain. Use the Subtraction Facts Chart (page 61) to demonstrate this to students. Enlarge and laminate the chart and cross off the groups they have learned with an overhead projector marker. Remaining facts will be taught in groups of number pairs.

9s: Ask students for addition problems in which the answer is nine:

8 + 1 = 9
7 + 2 = 9
6 + 3 = 9
5 + 4 = 9
4 + 5 = 9
3 + 6 = 9
2 + 7 = 9
1 + 8 = 9

The number pairs that equal nine are 8 and 1, 7 and 2, 6 and 3 and 4 and 5. Review these to help with nine minus a number. Ask for the subtraction facts made from these problems.

9 - 1 = 8
9 - 2 = 7
(9 - 3 = 6)
(9 - 4 = 5)
(9 - 5 = 4)
(9 - 6 = 3)
9 - 7 = 2
9 - 8 = 1

These answers can be checked on a number line. Also the travel folder has a row of 9 dots which can be used to check answers. Insert the travel folder into a vinyl page protector.

8s: Now ask for the addition problems in which 8 is the answer.

7 + 1 = 8
6 + 2 = 8
5 + 3 = 8
4 + 4 = 8
3 + 5 = 8
2 + 6 = 8
1 + 7 = 8

Now have the class give these as subtraction problems. Check the answers using a number line.

8 - 1 = 7
8 - 2 = 6
(8 - 3 = 5)
8 - 4 = 4
(8 - 5 = 3)
8 - 6 = 2
8 - 7 = 1

Ask students which ones have been learned in earlier lessons. All have been learned except 8 - 3 and 8 - 5. These will be learned now. They are matching facts.

Use a marker for overhead transparencies. For 9 - 1, draw a line below the top dot. Count the dots below the line. There are 8 and the answer is 9 - 1 = 8. For 9 - 2, clean off the first line and draw a line below the top two dots. Count the dots below the line. There are seven and the answer is 9 - 2 = 7.

All but four of these have already been learned in other lessons. 9 - 1 and 9 - 8 were taught in Lesson Plan 4, 9 - 2 and 9 - 7 were taught in Lesson Plan 7. The other four must be learned at this time. Students will learn them by studying the travel folder and reciting the facts as a group. Also flash cards and games will help students learn them by familiarity.

The four facts to be learned have been circled. Notice that they are pairs of matching facts.

LESSON PLAN 8

7s: Ask for the addition facts in which 7 is the answer.

6 + 1 = 7
5 + 2 = 7
4 + 3 = 7
3 + 4 = 7
2 + 5 = 7
1 + 6 = 7

Have the class give you these as subtraction facts. Check answers with a number line.

7 - 1 = 6
7 - 2 = 5
7 - 3 = 4
7 - 4 = 3
7 - 5 = 2
7 - 6 = 1

Ask the class which ones have been learned. All have been learned except 7 - 3 and 7 - 4.

Use practice facts sheets, travel folders and flash cards as described in earlier lessons.

ASSIGNMENT: Worksheets O and P.

For Worksheet P, show students that they can do subtraction in the 10s column the same way as in the 1s column. Use the Base 10 Counting Chart to demonstrate. Buy a large wall chart or enlarge and laminate the one in this book.

Example:

$$\begin{array}{r} 7 \\ -3 \\ \hline 4 \end{array}$$

$$\begin{array}{r} 70 \\ -30 \\ \hline ? \end{array}$$

Find 70 on the counting chart and count back 30 spaces. The answer is 40. If we covered the 0s, we could subtract 7 - 3 and get 4. Since the 7 and 3 are in the 10s place, they are groups of 10. We need the zero in the 1s place. We know that zero minus zero equals zero. Bring down the zero. This also shows that the answer is 40.

SOLITAIRE FOR NUMBER PAIRS: In the *Math Phonics™–Addition* book, there is a solitaire game which helps the students practice the number pairs for the more difficult addition facts. This same game is very helpful if used for these last units. For example, if they are playing solitaire for 9s, they practice 4 + 5 = 9. That helps them learn that 9 - 4 = 5 and 9 - 5 = 4. Instructions for the solitaire game are given on page 62.

SUBTRACTION FACTS CHART

−	0	1	2	3	4	5	6	7	8	9	10	11	12	13	14	15	16	17	18
0	0	1	2	3	4	5	6	7	8	9									
1		0	X	2	3	4	5	6	7	8	9								
2			0	1	X	3	4	5	6	7	8	9							
3				0	1	2	X	4	5	6	7	8	9						
4					0	1	2	3	X	5	6	7	8	9					
5						0	1	2	3	4	X	6	7	8	9				
6							0	1	2	3	4	5	X	7	8	9			
7								0	1	2	3	4	5	6	X	8	9		
8									0	1	2	3	4	5	6	7	X	9	
9										0	1	2	3	4	5	6	7	8	X
10											0								

0s

1s

2s

9s

9s Matching Facts

2s/Matching Facts

1s/Matching Facts

0s/Matching Facts

Xs are doubles.

SUBTRACTION FACTS CHART

−	0	1	2	3	4	5	6	7	8	9	10	11	12	13	14	15	16	17	18
0	0	1	2	3	4	5	6	7	8	9									
1		0	1	2	3	4	5	6	7	8	9								
2			0	1	2	3	4	5	6	7	8	9							
3				0	1	2	3	4	5	6	7	8	9						
4					0	1	2	3	4	5	6	7	8	9					
5						0	1	2	3	4	5	6	7	8	9				
6							0	1	2	3	4	5	6	7	8	9			
7								0	1	2	3	4	5	6	7	8	9		
8									0	1	2	3	4	5	6	7	8	9	
9										0	1	2	3	4	5	6	7	8	9
10											0								

NUMBER PAIR SOLITAIRE FOR 8s

The object of the game is to remove all cards faceup on the table by removing pairs of cards which equal 8.

1. Use a standard deck of playing cards. Remove 9s, 10s and face cards.
2. This is a one-player game, but students could play in pairs at first in order to learn the game.
3. Fifteen of the cards will be arranged in the shape of a triangle with the point of the triangle away from the player.
4. Put down the point card first. There are two cards in the second row, and they overlap the point card at its lower corners. There are three cards in the third row, and their corners overlap the corners of the two cards in row two. Each row overlaps lower corners of the row above. (See diagram.)
5. If two cards on the lower row equal eight, they are removed.
6. Student holds the remaining cards facedown in hand and turns over one at a time. Eights are automatically removed because 8 + 0 = 8.
7. If a card turned up in the hand can be paired with an uncovered card on the table to equal 8, both cards are removed.
8. If any two uncovered cards on the table can be paired to equal 8, remove them.
9. If necessary, have students use the Travel Folder for Number Pairs for 8 while playing Number Pair Solitaire for 8s to help them remember the number pairs.
10. Students go through the cards in hand once. To make the game easier, they could go through the cards more than

NOTE: This game can be played for each set of number pairs. The cards used will vary slightly, according to which numbers are added in the number pairs for each sum. For example, for the pairs for 14, here are the addition facts:

10 + 4 = 14
9 + 5 = 14
8 + 6 = 14
7 + 7 = 14

Therefore, the only cards needed for Addition Solitaire for the pairs for 14 are 4, 5, 6, 7, 8, 9 and 10.

Name ______________________

PRACTICE FACTS FOR NUMBER PAIRS FOR 7, 8 AND 9

7 - 1 = ______

7 - 2 = ______

7 - 3 = ______

7 - 4 = ______

7 - 5 = ______

7 - 6 = ______

7 - 7 = ______

8 - 1 = ______

8 - 2 = ______

8 - 3 = ______

8 - 4 = ______

8 - 5 = ______

8 - 6 = ______

8 - 7 = ______

8 - 8 = ______

9 - 1 = ______

9 - 2 = ______

9 - 3 = ______

9 - 4 = ______

9 - 5 = ______

9 - 6 = ______

9 - 7 = ______

9 - 8 = ______

9 - 9 = ______

Name ______________________________

TRAVEL FOLDER FOR NUMBER PAIRS FOR 7

7 - 1 = 6 7 - 1

7 - 2 = 5 7 - 2

7 - 3 = 4 7 - 3

7 - 4 = 3 7 - 4

7 - 5 = 2 7 - 5

7 - 6 = 1 7 - 6

Name ______________________________

TRAVEL FOLDER FOR NUMBER PAIRS FOR 8

8 - 1 = 7	8 - 1
8 - 2 = 6	8 - 2
8 - 3 = 5	8 - 3
8 - 4 = 4	8 - 4
8 - 5 = 3	8 - 5
8 - 6 = 2	8 - 6
8 - 7 = 1	8 - 7

Name ______________________

TRAVEL FOLDER FOR NUMBER PAIRS FOR 9

9 - 1 = 8 9 - 1

9 - 2 = 7 9 - 2

9 - 3 = 6 9 - 3

9 - 4 = 5 9 - 4

9 - 5 = 4 9 - 5

9 - 6 = 3 9 - 6

9 - 7 = 2 9 - 7

9 - 8 = 1 9 - 8

BASE 10 COUNTING CHART

1	2	3	4	5	6	7	8	9	10
11	12	13	14	15	16	17	18	19	20
21	22	23	24	25	26	27	28	29	30
31	32	33	34	35	36	37	38	39	40
41	42	43	44	45	46	47	48	49	50
51	52	53	54	55	56	57	58	59	60
61	62	63	64	65	66	67	68	69	70
71	72	73	74	75	76	77	78	79	80
81	82	83	84	85	86	87	88	89	90
91	92	93	94	95	96	97	98	99	100
101	102	103	104	105	106	107	108	109	110
111	112	113	114	115	116	117	118	119	120
121	122	123	124	125	126	127	128	129	130
131	132	133	134	135	136	137	138	139	140
141	142	143	144	145	146	147	148	149	150

Name ______________________

7s, 8s AND 9s

1. 7 - 7	2. 7 - 1	3. 8 - 1	4. 7 - 3	5. 8 - 4
6. 7 - 2	7. 8 - 2	8. 7 - 4	9. 8 - 5	10. 9 - 3
11. 8 - 3	12. 7 - 5	13. 8 - 6	14. 9 - 6	15. 9 - 7
16. 7 - 6	17. 8 - 7	18. 9 - 5	19. 9 - 2	20. 9 - 4

21. Karen raises sheep. She has 9 sheep. Six ran away. How many sheep are left?

22. She found 2 of the lost sheep. Now how many sheep does she have that are found?

CHALLENGE:

1. She is still missing the 4 runaway sheep. Her uncle gave her 2 dozen more. Two were sick, so he took them back. Now what is her total?
2. She has 16 sheep which need to have their hooves cleaned. How many hooves will need to be cleaned?
3. It costs 2 dollars to clean one hoof. How much will it cost to have the hooves of 16 sheep cleaned?

Name ______________________________

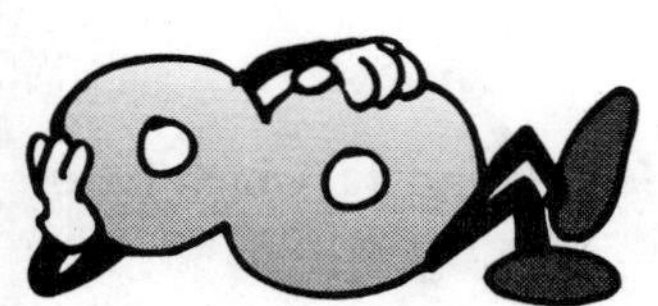

7s, 8s AND 9s

1. 70 − 10	2. 80 − 10	3. 70 − 70	4. 70 − 30	5. 80 − 40
6. 70 − 20	7. 80 − 20	8. 70 − 40	9. 80 − 50	10. 90 − 30
11. 80 − 30	12. 70 − 50	13. 80 − 60	14. 90 − 60	15. 90 − 70
16. 70 − 60	17. 80 − 70	18. 90 − 50	19. 90 − 20	20. 90 − 40

Review

21. 80 − 20	22. 60 − 40	23. 160 − 70	24. 70 − 50	25. 30 − 10
26. 140 − 50	27. 70 − 20	28. 80 − 60	29. 90 − 70	30. 100 − 20

LESSON PLAN 9

OBJECTIVE: Number pairs for 10 and 11. Students will be shown the number pairs for 10 and 11 which have not already been taught.

MATERIALS: Flash Cards (pages 21-28), Practice Facts for 10s and 11s (page 71), Travel Folder for Number Pairs for 10 (page 72), Travel Folder for Number Pairs for 11 (page 73), Worksheets Q and R (pages 74 and 75)

INTRODUCTION: Have the class chant the subtraction number pairs for seven, eight and nine. Chant other groups until students have mastered them. Pick out facts at random–you give the fact and have the class call out the answer. Review rules.

REVIEW: Ask students for addition problems in which the answer is 10.

9 + 1 = 10
8 + 2 = 10
7 + 3 = 10
6 + 4 = 10
5 + 5 = 10
4 + 6 = 10
3 + 7 = 10
2 + 8 = 10
1 + 9 = 10

Now have the class give these as subtraction problems. Check the answers using a number line.

10 - 1 = 9
10 - 2 = 8
(10 - 3 = 7
10 - 4 = 6)
10 - 5 = 5
(10 - 6 = 4
10 - 7 = 3)
10 - 8 = 2
10 - 9 = 1

Show the students on a number line that these are correct. Also, use the dots on the travel folder to demonstrate these. See Lesson Plan 8 (page 58) for instructions on how to use the dots. Ask students which of these have already been learned. All but four of these facts have been learned in earlier groups, and the four are matching facts of each other. The four to be learned have been circled.

ASSIGNMENT: Worksheets Q and R.

11s: Go through the same process with the 11s. Here are the addition facts.

9 + 2 = 11
8 + 3 = 11
7 + 4 = 11
6 + 5 = 11
5 + 6 = 11
4 + 7 = 11
3 + 8 = 11
2 + 9 = 11

Ask students for the matching subtraction facts.

11 - 2 = 9
(11 - 3 = 8
11 - 4 = 7
11 - 5 = 6
11 - 6 = 5
11 - 7 = 4
11 - 8 = 3)
11 - 9 = 2

All but six have already been learned. The six new facts have been circled, and they are matching facts of each other. Use the dots on the travel folder to demonstrate these facts.

Use practice facts sheet, travel folders and flash cards as described in earlier lessons.

GAME: Playing cards flash cards.

Use a standard deck of cards. Remove the face cards. One person can do this for practice, or two can play a contest.

Divide cards into two piles. Leave facedown. Turn over the top card from each pile. Use the two numbers to make one or more subtraction facts–give the correct answer.

If two people play, they could take turns, or the first to call out the correct answer could get the cards.

Name ______________________________

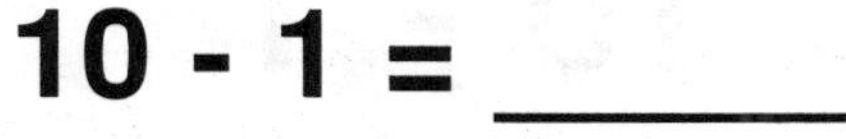

PRACTICE FACTS FOR 10s AND 11s

10 - 1 = ______

10 - 2 = ______

10 - 3 = ______

10 - 4 = ______

10 - 5 = ______

10 - 6 = ______

10 - 7 = ______

10 - 8 = ______

10 - 9 = ______

11 - 1 = ______

11 - 2 = ______

11 - 3 = ______

11 - 4 = ______

11 - 5 = ______

11 - 6 = ______

11 - 7 = ______

11 - 8 = ______

11 - 9 = ______

Name ______________________________

TRAVEL FOLDER FOR NUMBER PAIRS FOR 10

10 - 1 = 9	10 - 1
10 - 2 = 8	10 - 2
10 - 3 = 7	10 - 3
10 - 4 = 6	10 - 4
10 - 5 = 5	10 - 5
10 - 6 = 4	10 - 6
10 - 7 = 3	10 - 7
10 - 8 = 2	10 - 8
10 - 9 = 1	10 - 9

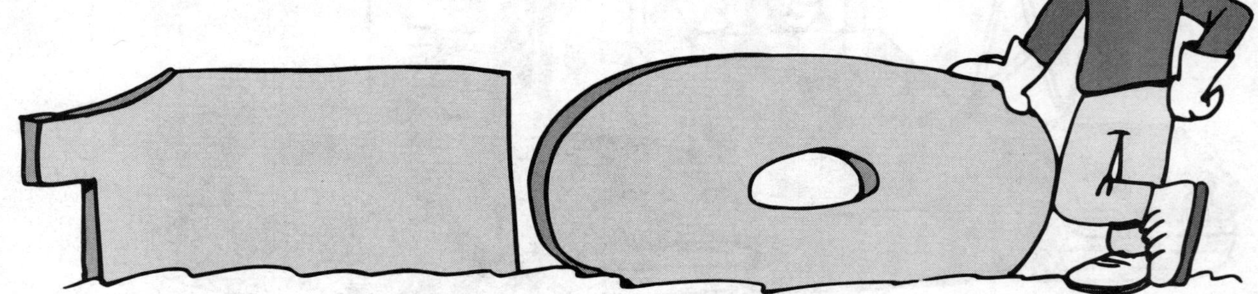

Name ______________________________

TRAVEL FOLDER FOR NUMBER PAIRS FOR 11

11 - 2 = 9   11 - 2

11 - 3 = 8   11 - 3

11 - 4 = 7   11 - 4

11 - 5 = 6   11 - 5

11 - 6 = 5   11 - 6

11 - 7 = 4   11 - 7

11 - 8 = 3   11 - 8

11 - 9 = 2   11 - 9

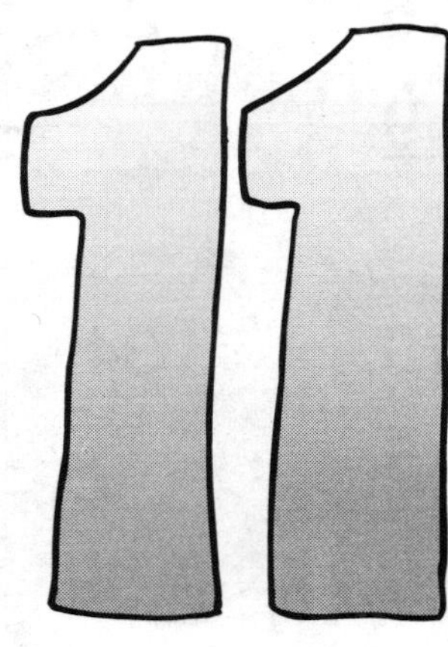

Name ______________________________ **WORKSHEET Q**

10s AND 11s

1. 10 - 6	2. 11 - 1	3. 10 - 1	4. 11 - 4	5. 10 - 3
6. 11 - 7	7. 10 - 5	8. 11 - 5	9. 10 - 2	10. 11 - 6
11. 10 - 7	12. 11 - 8	13. 10 - 4	14. 11 - 3	15. 10 - 9
16. 10 - 10	17. 11 - 9	18. 10 - 8	19. 11 - 0	20. 11 - 2

Review

21. 13 - 9	22. 8 - 2	23. 10 - 2	24. 11 - 3	25. 17 - 9
26. 17 - 8	27. 7 - 2	28. 16 - 9	29. 15 - 9	30. 16 - 7
31. 8 - 5	32. 15 - 7	33. 10 - 6	34. 11 - 6	35. 10 - 7

Name ______________________________

WORKSHEET R

HEXAGON WORK

Subtract each smaller number from the number in the center. Write the answer in the large space. See the example in the first problem: 8 - 2 = 6.

1.

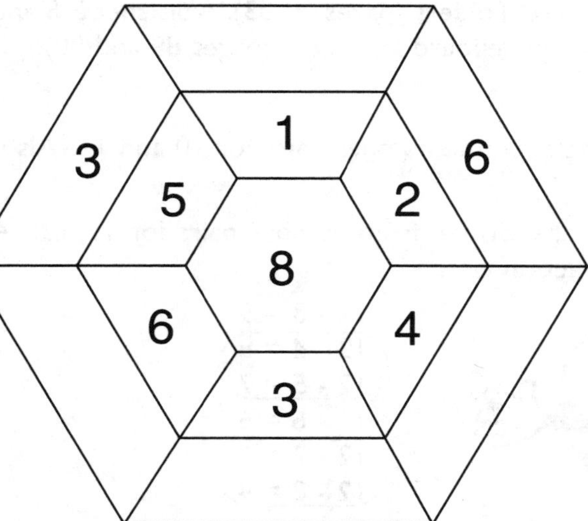

2.

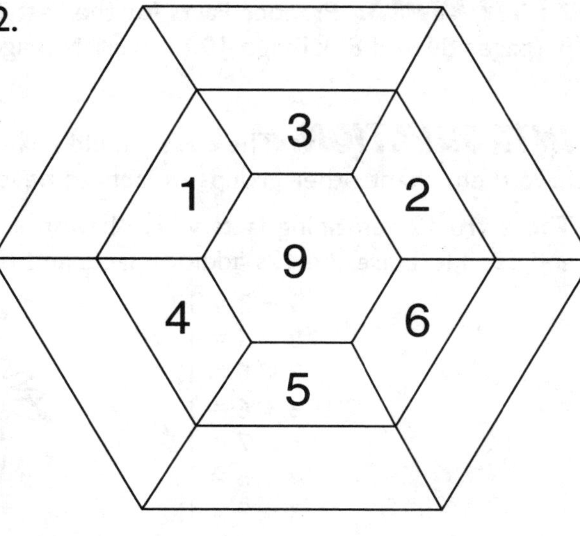

3.

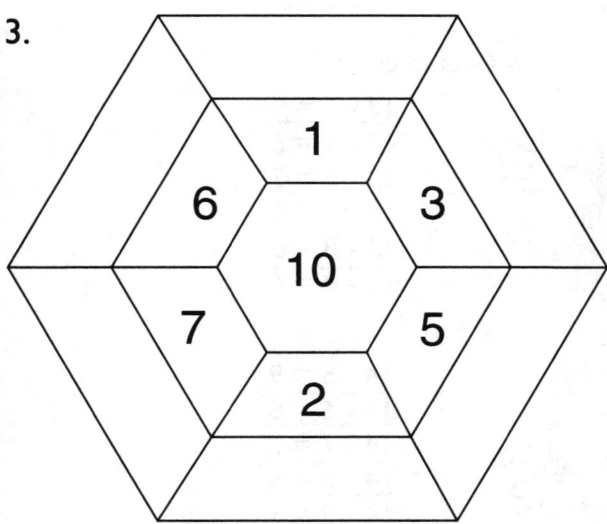

4.

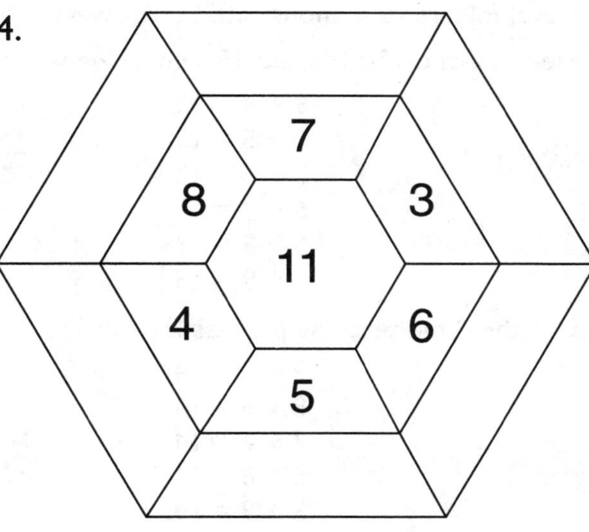

5. Juan has one nickel and one dime. He spends 4¢. How much money does he have left?

CHALLENGE:
Juan finds two nickels and two dimes. He puts this with his change. Does he have enough for a 35¢ baseball card?

LESSON PLAN 10

OBJECTIVE: Last 12 facts. Students will be shown the 12 facts that have not yet been taught.

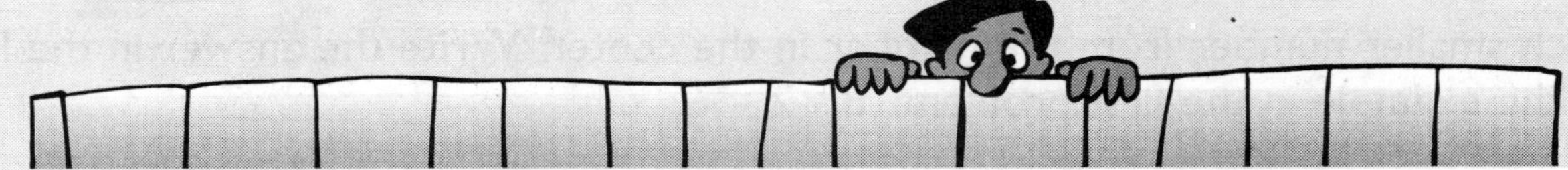

MATERIALS: Practice Facts for the Last 12 Facts (page 79), Travel Folders (pages 80-83), Worksheets S and T (pages 84 and 85), Bingo 100 materials (pages 86-88), Math Path gameboard and cards (pages 89 and 90)

INTRODUCTION: The class should chant the subtraction facts for the number pairs for 10 and 11. Also, have them chant other groups of facts as needed. Review rules.

There are 12 remaining facts which have not been taught. They are formed from number pairs for 12, 13, 14 and 15. Here are the 12s addition facts and their matching subtraction facts.

9 + 3 = 12	12 - 3 = 9
8 + 4 = 12	(12 - 4 = 8)
7 + 5 = 12	(12 - 5 = 7)
6 + 6 = 12	12 - 6 = 6
5 + 7 = 12	(12 - 7 = 5)
4 + 8 = 12	(12 - 8 = 4)
3 + 9 = 12	12 - 9 = 3

To keep things simple, we will omit 12 - 1 and 12 - 2 since they really were taught with 2 - 1 and 2 - 2. Also, it is not necessary to cover 12 - 10 because that really is subtracting 2 - 0 and 1 - 1. The subtraction facts that have not already been taught have been circled.

Use practice facts and travel folders to teach these facts. Students could make their own. Use the dots on the travel folders to demonstrate the answers.

Here are the 13s, 14s and 15s which we will cover at this time with new facts circled.

9 + 4 = 13	13 - 4 = 9
8 + 5 = 13	(13 - 5 = 8)
7 + 6 = 13	(13 - 6 = 7)
6 + 7 = 13	(13 - 7 = 6)
5 + 8 = 13	(13 - 8 = 5)
4 + 9 = 13	13 - 9 = 4

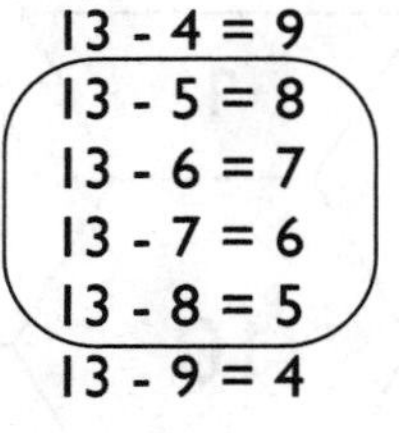

Use the same teaching process for the 13s.

9 + 5 = 14	14 - 5 = 9
8 + 6 = 14	(14 - 6 = 8)
7 + 7 = 14	14 - 7 = 7
6 + 8 = 14	(14 - 8 = 6)
5 + 9 = 14	14 - 9 = 5

Use the same process for teaching 14s.

9 + 6 = 15	15 - 6 = 9
8 + 7 = 15	(15 - 7 = 8)
7 + 8 = 15	(15 - 8 = 7)
6 + 9 = 15	15 - 9 = 6

Use the same process for teaching 15s.

LESSON PLAN 10

MATH PATH GAME: The Math Path Game can be played on the gameboard included in this lesson plan. Enlarge and laminate if you will be using it in the classroom. You may want to send a game home with each student. If so, they do not need to be enlarged. Use coins or any small objects as movers. Cut apart the cards on page 90.

You will need two six-sided solids for this game. Two standard dice will work if you cover the spots with small stickers and write numbers on the stickers. One die should have the numbers 4, 5, 6, 7, 8 and 9 and the other should have 9, 10, 11, 12, 13 and 14.

A student should roll the two dice, subtract the two numbers and give the answer. The answer tells them how many spaces they can move. Use the Subtraction Facts sheet on page 9 to check for correct answers. It is okay for two movers to be on the same space. At the end of this game, you do not have to have the exact number to win. For example, if you are three spaces from the A+ and you get to move five spaces, you can still go out.

The purpose of this game is to give students practice with some of the more difficult subtraction problems, review some of the more difficult addition facts and practice some of the easier multiplication facts.

NOTE: Each Times and Plus card has bullets (•) which help students find the correct answer. If students give the correct answer on a Plus or Times card, they can move ahead two more spaces.

JUST FOR FUN: Have students say the name Math Path 10 times as fast as they can. Save this for the end of class when you don't mind if they get a little silly!

BINGO 100: The object of this game is to teach students to make change for a dollar quickly and accurately. You may want to use this later in the year when students have had practice subtracting two columns of numbers. However, you can teach that right now and use the two-column Worksheets U and V (pages 87 and 88) and practice facts for a little advance practice. Then play the game from time to time for drill.

If bingo cards are laminated, students can cross off each number with a crayon, thus eliminating the need for something like beans or squares of paper to cover the numbers. This makes this a less messy game. When each game is over, students clean off the crayon Xs by rubbing with a dry facial tissue.

LESSON PLAN 10

BEGINNERS BINGO 100: Start out with numbers divisible by five. Give each student a 4" x 4" (10 x 10 cm) grid found in Lesson Plan 6. Have them fill in numbers one day, then laminate the cards and play the game later. Each grid gets one free space located wherever the student chooses. Ask students to count by 5s from 0 to 100 and write those numbers on the board. Students should choose from those numbers to fill in the squares of the grid.

When you call out a number–say 25–they will cover the number representing the change they would get back from a dollar.

Demonstrate 100 - 25 using the Base 10 Counting Chart. Then show the concept of borrowing or regrouping.

Example: 100
-25

The 100 is 10 groups of 10. Show them this on the Base 10 Counting Chart. We can take one group of 10 and use it to subtract the 5. This leaves 9 groups of 10 to use for subtracting the two.

9 10
~~10~~0
-25
75

Now the answer is 75–the answer we got when counting backwards on the Base 10 Counting Chart. Do a few more examples and assign the worksheets.

ADVANCED BINGO 100: Use regular bingo cards. Laminate them and let students use crayons to X out numbers.

This game will let students practice subtracting all numbers–not just those divisible by five. Since numbers on the bingo cards go from 1-75, you can call out any number from 25 to 99. Copy a Base 10 Counting Chart, cut out the numbers and use the numbers from 25 to 99 to pull out of a box when calling the bingo numbers. Practice a few of the problems as described above, give the worksheet for practice, and play the game from time to time.

Copy these two pages and send home to parents so they can play these games at home with their children.

Hint: Many times people make the mistake of thinking that 100 - 44 = 66 because 10 - 4 = 6. They forget that they had to borrow from the 10s and that makes the answer 100 - 44 = 56. Point this out to students so they can think of answers quickly. It's much easier when they are subtracting a number ending with zero: 100 - 30 = 70 because 10 - 3 = 7.

Name ________________________________

PRACTICE FACTS FOR THE LAST 12 FACTS

12 - 3 = ______

12 - 4 = ______

12 - 5 = ______

12 - 6 = ______

12 - 7 = ______

12 - 8 = ______

12 - 9 = ______

13 - 4 = ______

13 - 5 = ______

13 - 6 = ______

13 - 7 = ______

13 - 8 = ______

13 - 9 = ______

14 - 5 = ______

14 - 6 = ______

14 - 7 = ______

14 - 8 = ______

14 - 9 = ______

15 - 6 = ______

15 - 7 = ______

15 - 8 = ______

15 - 9 = ______

Name ______________________________

TRAVEL FOLDER FOR NUMBER PAIRS FOR 12

12 - 3 = 9   12 - 3

12 - 4 = 8   12 - 4

12 - 5 = 7   12 - 5

12 - 6 = 6   12 - 6

12 - 7 = 5   12 - 7

12 - 8 = 4   12 - 8

12 - 9 = 3   12 - 9

Name ______________________________

TRAVEL FOLDER FOR NUMBER PAIRS FOR 13

13 - 4 = 9   13 - 4

13 - 5 = 8   13 - 5

13 - 6 = 7   13 - 6

13 - 7 = 6   13 - 7

13 - 8 = 5   13 - 8

13 - 9 = 4   13 - 9

Name ______________________________

TRAVEL FOLDER FOR NUMBER PAIRS FOR 14

14 - 5 = 9   14 - 5

14 - 6 = 8   14 - 6

14 - 7 = 7   14 - 7

14 - 8 = 6   14 - 8

14 - 9 = 5   14 - 9

Name ______________________________

TRAVEL FOLDER FOR NUMBER PAIRS FOR 15

15 - 6 = 9	15 - 6
15 - 7 = 8	15 - 7
15 - 8 = 7	15 - 8
15 - 9 = 6	15 - 9

Name ______________________________

LAST 12 FACTS

1. 12 − 3	2. 13 − 4	3. 14 − 5	4. 12 − 4	5. 13 − 6
6. 14 − 5	7. 13 − 9	8. 14 − 8	9. 12 − 5	10. 13 − 7
11. 12 − 8	12. 13 − 4	13. 12 − 6	14. 15 − 7	15. 13 − 8
16. 15 − 8	17. 12 − 7	18. 14 − 6	19. 12 − 9	20. 13 − 5

21. It's two full weeks until the end of school. How many days in all?
22. Take away two weekends and how many school days are left?
23. There will be no homework on the last two days of school. How many days of homework are left?

CHALLENGE:
There are three homework assignments each day. How many homework assignments in all?

Name ______________________________

REVIEW

1. 10 - 3	2. 12 - 3	3. 11 - 2	4. 13 - 5	5. 14 - 6
6. 13 - 4	7. 10 - 4	8. 12 - 4	9. 11 - 3	10. 13 - 7
11. 11 - 5	12. 14 - 8	13. 10 - 6	14. 12 - 5	15. 11 - 4
16. 15 - 7	17. 11 - 6	18. 13 - 8	19. 10 - 7	20. 12 - 7
21. 12 - 8	22. 13 - 6	23. 11 - 7	24. 14 - 5	25. 10 - 8

26. On the last day of school, 13 kids brought treats. Six brought cupcakes. How many did not bring cupcakes?

CHALLENGE:
Each cupcake person brought one dozen cupcakes. How many cupcakes were there in all?

PRACTICE FACTS FOR BINGO 100 FOR BEGINNERS

100 - 5 = ________

100 - 10 = ________

100 - 15 = ________

100 - 20 = ________

100 - 25 = ________

100 - 30 = ________

100 - 35 = ________

100 - 40 = ________

100 - 45 = ________

100 - 50 = ________

Name the matching fact for each problem.

Name ______________________

BINGO 100 FOR BEGINNERS

1. 100 - 25	2. 100 - 30	3. 100 - 5	4. 100 - 20
5. 100 - 60	6. 100 - 75	7. 100 - 10	8. 100 - 45
9. 100 - 40	10. 100 - 55	11. 100 - 50	12. 100 - 70
13. 100 - 65	14. 100 - 85	15. 100 - 80	16. 100 - 35
17. 100 - 55	18. 100 - 90	19. 100 - 95	20. 100 - 15
21. 100 - 75	22. 100 - 40	23. 100 - 35	24. 100 - 20

25. James had a dollar. He spent 60¢. What was his change?
26. Emil bought two candy bars costing 35¢ each. What was his change from a dollar?

Name ______________________________

BINGO 100 FOR ALL NUMBERS

1. 100 - 99
2. 100 - 27
3. 100 - 33
4. 100 - 42
5. 100 - 63
6. 100 - 57
7. 100 - 97
8. 100 - 29
9. 100 - 82
10. 100 - 36
11. 100 - 64
12. 100 - 67
13. 100 - 54
14. 100 - 96
15. 100 - 37
16. 100 - 47
17. 100 - 89
18. 100 - 83
19. 100 - 93
20. 100 - 51
21. 100 - 43
22. 100 - 46
23. 100 - 57
24. 100 - 92

25. If you spent 53¢, what would your change from a dollar be?

CHALLENGE:
Your class can spend $100.00 on supplies for your classroom. If you spend $33.00 on paint and $42.00 on art paper, how much money is left?

MATH PATH

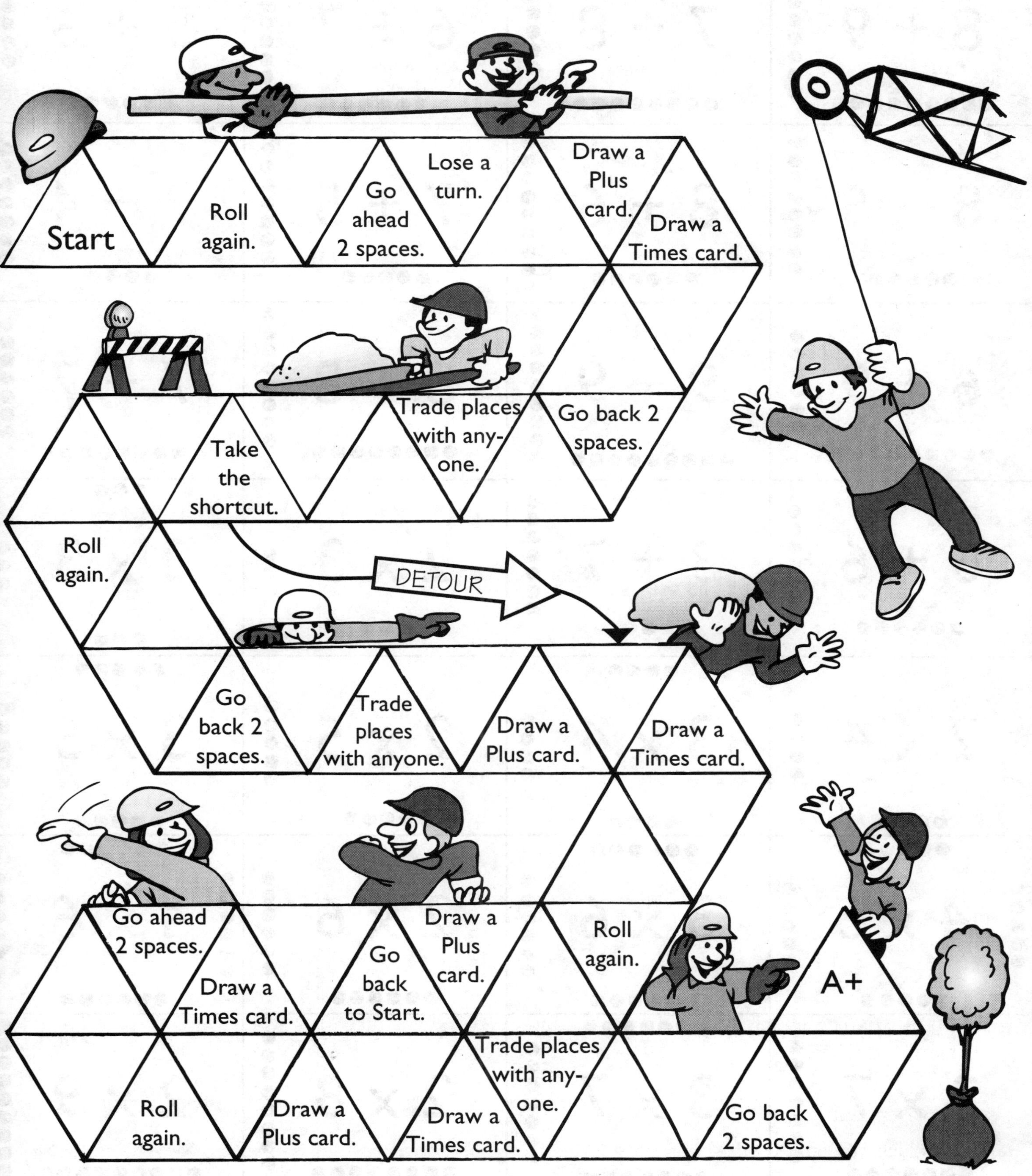
Start
Roll again.
Go ahead 2 spaces.
Lose a turn.
Draw a Plus card.
Draw a Times card.
Go back 2 spaces.
Trade places with any-one.
Take the shortcut.
Roll again.
DETOUR
Go back 2 spaces.
Trade places with anyone.
Draw a Plus card.
Draw a Times card.
Go ahead 2 spaces.
Draw a Times card.
Go back to Start.
Draw a Plus card.
Roll again.
A+
Roll again.
Draw a Plus card.
Draw a Times card.
Trade places with any-one.
Go back 2 spaces.

8 + 9	7 + 8	6 + 7	5 + 6
8 + 5	8 + 6	7 + 5	7 + 4
6 + 9	9 + 9	8 + 8	7 + 7
6 + 6	3 + 7	2 x 3	3 x 3
2 x 4	3 x 4	2 x 5	3 x 5
4 x 5	3 x 6	2 x 6	4 x 6
2 x 7	3 x 7	2 x 8	2 x 9

REVIEW AND ASSESSMENT

If you have followed the instructions in this book, each student will have a folder with materials for reviewing all the subtraction facts.

Collect the Student's Math Phonics™ Progress Charts (page 32) and record student progress on the Teacher's Math Phonics™ Progress Chart (page 33). Go over any areas that students still need to study. Review pages make good quizzes. A page with several T-table charts also makes a good quiz.

Classroom games are a good way to practice and drill. Have students write the facts they miss five times each.

Use the assessment pages like a test to check students' progress. Highlight the ones that are correct. Also, give students a copy of page 9 and have them highlight the ones they got correct on the assessment. Have students practice the ones they have missed and take the assessment again.

RULES AND GAMES

Give each student a copy of the rules and games (page 92) to keep and study. Enlarge and laminate the rules part of the page and post it in the classroom. Refer to the rules to remind students how easy it is to subtract.

RULES AND GAMES

SUBTRACTION: A way of keeping track of how many objects we have after some have been removed.

ADDITION: The three numbers in an addition problem can be used to make one or two subtraction problems.

EVENS AND ODDS: An even number is any number which ends in 0, 2, 4, 6 or 8. An odd number is any number which ends in 1, 3, 5, 7 or 9.

NUMBER NEIGHBORS: When you subtract a smaller number neighbor from a larger one, the answer is one.

1s: When you subtract one from a number, the answer is the smaller number neighbor.

9s: When you subtract nine from a teens number, add the two numerals of the teens number. That is the answer.

When you have a number in the teens and in the 1s column, you are subtracting a larger number neighbor from a smaller one, the answer is nine.

2s: When you subtract two from an odd number, the answer is the next smaller odd number.

When you subtract two from an even number, the answer is the next smaller even number.

When you subtract two closest odd numbers, the answer is two.

When you subtract two closest even numbers, the answer is two.

GAMES

TRIVIAL PURSUIT™: Use flash cards as question cards. Play according to the rules.

QUIZ BOWL: This will be played at school. Instructions are found in Lesson Plan 4 (page 34).

DOMINO FLASH CARDS: Dominoes are facedown. Turn one faceup. Make a subtraction problem, subtracting the smaller number of spots from the larger number. For a two-player game, players take turns turning up a domino. If the player gives the correct answer, he keeps the domino. Check Subtraction Facts (page 9) for correct answers.

SUBTRACTION BINGO: Use flash cards (page 21-28) which students are studying. Call out the problem–students cover the answer on their card.

DICE FLASH CARDS: Use two standard dice. Roll the dice. Subtract the smaller number from a larger number. Give answer.

ADDITION SOLITAIRE: Instructions on page 62.

PLAYING CARD FLASH CARDS: Remove face cards. Divide cards into two equal piles. Turn over the top card of each pile. Make a subtraction fact from the two numbers. One- or two-player game, the first player to call out the correct answer keeps the two cards.

MATH PATH GAME: Instructions on page 77.

BINGO 100: Instructions on pages 77 and 78.

Name ______________________________

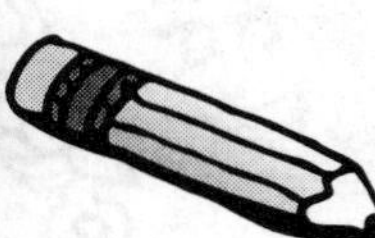

SUBTRACTION ASSESSMENT

1. 7 - 6	2. 9 - 7	3. 18 - 9	4. 3 - 3	5. 11 - 7
6. 12 - 6	7. 8 - 6	8. 13 - 4	9. 10 - 4	10. 16 - 7
11. 8 - 4	12. 11 - 2	13. 2 - 2	14. 17 - 8	15. 15 - 8
16. 1 - 1	17. 10 - 9	18. 7 - 2	19. 9 - 4	20. 6 - 4
21. 12 - 3	22. 8 - 1	23. 4 - 3	24. 14 - 6	25. 17 - 9
26. 12 - 9	27. 12 - 8	28. 14 - 5	29. 8 - 7	30. 13 - 5
31. 5 - 3	32. 5 - 4	33. 13 - 6	34. 11 - 5	35. 9 - 4
36. 5 - 1	37. 9 - 9	38. 16 - 9	39. 11 - 6	40. 10 - 8
41. 14 - 9	42. 5 - 5	43. 14 - 7	44. 13 - 8	45. 7 - 5
46. 9 - 8	47. 7 - 1	48. 5 - 2	49. 6 - 3	50. 6 - 6

Name ______________________________

SUBTRACTION ASSESSMENT

51. 10 - 6	52. 11 - 7	53. 10 -10	54. 12 - 4	55. 2 - 1
56. 11 - 3	57. 3 - 0	58. 10 - 7	59. 4 - 4	60. 10 - 3
61. 9 - 1	62. 9 - 0	63. 2 - 0	64. 16 - 8	65. 1 - 0
66. 12 - 1	67. 15 - 6	68. 15 - 9	69. 8 - 8	70. 8 - 2
71. 0 - 0	72. 12 - 7	73. 14 - 8	74. 9 - 3	75. 11 - 8
76. 10 - 5	77. 9 - 6	78. 9 - 8	79. 13 - 7	80. 7 - 7
81. 8 - 5	82. 7 - 4	83. 6 - 0	84. 13 - 9	85. 4 - 1
86. 5 - 0	87. 6 - 5	88. 8 - 3	89. 11 - 9	90. 6 - 1
91. 15 - 7	92. 3 - 1	93. 6 - 2	94. 4 - 0	95. 8 - 0

96. 10 - 2	97. 10 - 1	98. 3 - 2	99. 7 - 0	100. 7 - 3	101. 4 - 2

ANSWER KEY

Worksheet A, page 12

Challenge: 97

Worksheet B, page 18

Challenge:

a. 33	77	b. 27	99	c. 66	99	d. 55	77
+44	-33	+72	-27	+33	-33	+22	-22
77	44	99	72	99	66	77	55

Worksheet C, page 19

Challenge: 14

Worksheet D, page 31

```
R N B S T O N A X E S T Z L
A B X U S T O D A R N P E S
S T U B A L T D O L N I R T
M U L T I P L I C A T I O N
Q O N R T L B T S N X Z Y T
T O N A R P D I V I S I O N
S U P C L Y S O E N U T R Y
F A C T O R Q N R P M S T O
D Y S I N M U S T X M L P Z
A E I O U N I L U S T E R Y
P O N N U M B E R S C R G Y
```

Challenge: 80

Worksheet E, page 37

Challenge: 34

Worksheet F, page 38

Challenge: 12

Worksheet G, page 41

How do cows do their shopping? By catalog

Worksheet H, page 43

Challenge: 51

Worksheet J, page 48

Challenge: 22

Worksheet L, page 55

Challenge: yellow

Worksheet O, page 68

Challenge: 1. 27, 2. 64, 3. $128

Worksheet R, page 75

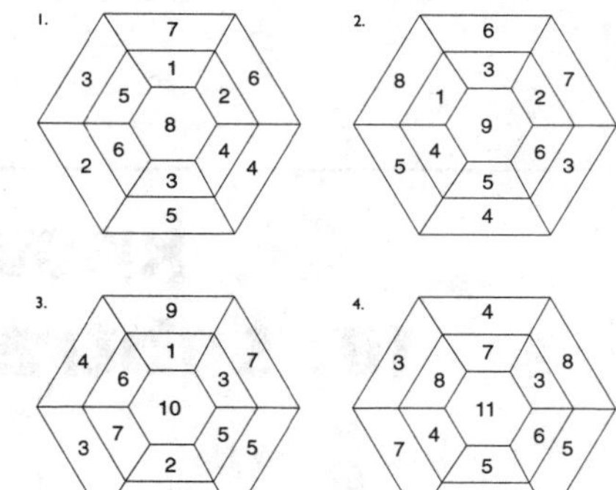

Challenge: yes

Worksheet S, page 84

Challenge: 24

Worksheet T, page 85

Challenge: 72

Worksheet V, page 88

Challenge: $25

CONGRATULATIONS!

knows the
101 subtraction facts.

signed

date

CONGRATULATIONS!

YOU ARE A

SUBTRACTION

MASTER!

signed

date